# SOUTH ASIAN MARGIINAL

# CONTEXT OF *THE GOD OF SMALL THINGS* AND *THE BRIDE*

## ALIA BASHIR

**DEDICATION**

To my mother

# Contents

# Preface

**ACKNOWLEDGEMENTS**

Chapter - I

Introduction                     1-5

Chapter - II

Literature Review            6-34

Chapter - III

Research Methodology     35-43

Chapter – IV

Results, Analysis and Discussion
44-91

Chapter V

Conclusions                    92-98

Bibliography                   99-103

**Preface:**

Marginality is a universal phenomenon. No known civilization, whether Eastern or Western, has been unaware of the structures of power related to the politics of the center and the margin. Women have been marginalized from mainstream political and social concerns. The voice against this discrimination was first raised in Europe. But the phenomenon of marginalization of women is more pronounced in South Asian context. The purpose of this book is to highlight the reasons as to why South Asian society is particularly exposed to the politics of the center and the margin. In order to address this issue, I have selected *The God of Small Things* (1997) and *The Bride* (1982) by prominent female novelists from South Asia, i.e. Arundhati Roy and Bapsi Sidwa. These texts have been isolated on the basis of cultural and economic oppression of female characters in the novels. The texts have been placed in the larger context of South Asia and have been studied through comparative approach as to why South Asian societies have these features in common. Similarly, South Asian social structure has also been studied through another perspective, such as from the viewpoint of Showalter and Spivak, which helps to determine the difference between the

Eastern and Western feminism. Unit analysis or close reading method has been employed to highlight important passages from the texts to show that female characters in the novels are marginalized in social and political concerns. Marxist theoretical perspective has been employed to solve the research questions. The study will be helpful in comparative understanding of the novels. Marginalization of women can be minimized by giving them equal access to resources.

Alia Bashir

## Acknowledgements:

I am grateful to Dr.Adil and my husband Ahsan-ur Rahim who gave me inspiration to write and publish this work.

Thanks to Sarmad and Amn, my dear children and my mother-in-law

for their love and encouragement.

Chapter One

**Introduction**

Women, the world over, have been marginalized from mainstream social and political concerns. They have been deprived of their due rights; social, political, legal, economic and religious (Gonsalves, 2011). This politics of the center and the margin which has been working in the form of various forces, e.g. imperialism and neo imperialism and of patriarchy and colonial rule, establish, women, as the marginalized part of the society. Although this phenomenon has long been the part of world politics, whether it has been the European, African or Asian civilization, South Asian societies are more exposed to the politics of center. Such marginalized position of women in South Asian context, is to be located not only in different economic forces working in South Asia, but also at its multicultural, postcolonial social structure; cultural forces in the societies of India and Pakistan are equally responsible for women's marginalization. Therefore, the 'women's question' in South Asian context is double edged: the question of pre-colonial customs and of postcolonial laws and their effects on the rights of women.

In order to solve the query as to why South Asian women are marginalized in the context of their rights, I carried out my research on two novels, *The God of Small Things* and *The Bride*, both from South

Asian women novelists, Arundhati Roy and Bapsi Sidwa. A striking commonality between these two novels is the presence of economic and cultural oppression which has been set in the backdrop of multicultural societies. All of the female characters are set in their struggle for equality. This research work critically studies their marginalized position from various perspectives; social, legal, political, religious and economics. Especially focusing on the economic issues, independent economic rights, ownership and the control of property at the hands of women, this research work also traces the history of disinheritance of women in South Asian societies. Another perspective through which the novels have been studied is the depiction of suppressed female characters in multicultural, postcolonial societies and how far cultural assimilation, a prominent feature in Indian and Pakistani context, could have been responsible for female oppression in the novels.

The journey of self-identity undertaken by women in global as well as South Asian context has been studied through the lens of Western characters present in novels in question. Although sharing the same sisterhood throughout the world, there is a visible difference between the degree of change which the Western and the South Asian women are taking. The commonalities as well as the diversities existing between the Western and Eastern feminism have been studied in order to explore as to why South Asian belt is particularly exposed to the marginalizing forces of patriarchy, imperialism, neo-imperialism and globalization, and what makes the South Asian women writers, in our context, Arundhati Roy and Bapsi Sidwa, protest against the institutionalization of marginalization. At the end, the question as to whether economic base is the driving force for female oppression or the superstructure or culture, it generates; and how far that cultural oppression is changeable with the passage of time. In other words, why do Roy and Sidwa place economic and cultural oppression side by side? From the above overview, following research questions have been raised:

1. Why South Asian society is particularly exposed to marginalization?
2. How far economic rights in particular and social, political, legal and religious rights in general could have determined the rightful status of female characters in the novels *The God of Small Things* and *The Bride*?
3. How far cultural assimilation, in the context of *The God of Small Things* and *The Bride* could have been responsible for marginalizing women?

4. Whether female subordination in the novels is due to cultural oppression or due to the material base of the society?

While going through the novels, *The God of Small Things* and *The Bride,* what is noticeable at the very outset is the economic oppression of female characters, e.g. Mammachi, Baby Kochamma, Ammu and Rahel are economically deprived. Similarly, the female characters in *The Bride*, especially the depiction of the women from the dancing culture, are also the manifestation of economic deprivation. The resonance of Locust Stand I or *locus standi* and the commoditization of women in the novels testifies to the fact that women's lack of access to the resources is, in fact, the reason of their deprived status. Empowering women can minimize their marginalization from all spheres. In the same line of thought, the presumption that culture is responsible for marginalization of women, the economic perspective of marginalization has largely been ignored. It is this context, the economic deprivation, in my view, that Roy and Sidwa systematically reveal in their depiction of the female characters and it is this rationale that motivates the researcher to carry out this research work.

Organization of the study:

This study is divided into five chapters.

Chapter I:

Chapter I offers the introduction of the area of research i.e. marginalization of South Asian women in the context of *The God of Small Things* and *The Bride*. This chapter briefly highlights the research questions, rationale, significance of the study, methodology and organization of the study.

Chapter II:

Following the Introduction chapter is the literature review which highlights the research undertaken previously, an in-depth account of the background literature and the niche which has largely remained unnoticed. This chapter not only provides the overview of the work undertaken on *The God of Small*

*Things* and *The Bride* but also provides the work done on South Asia from different perspectives relevant to the present research, i.e. hierarchal structure of India and Pakistan, e.g. the divide between rich and poor or class and caste; the gender issues; the impact of culture in postcolonial societies of South Asia and its effects on the economic and social lives of women. Literature review also includes the critical perspective through which various critics, such as Showalter and Spivak, Western as well as Eastern, have understood the gendered concept of womanhood and the implication of different cultures on gender issues; hence, giving an account of different womanhood of South Asian postcolonial societies.

Chapter III:

Methodology describes the framework through which the research problem has been approached and theoretical perspective through which the problem of marginalization of female characters has been handled. Important passages on social, political, legal and economic marginalization have been highlighted from the text through unit analysis or close reading method. As the research problem underpins the rights of women in a postcolonial society, Marxist theoretical perspective with its various interpretations, political, social and economic; the postcolonial, Subaltern Marxist perspective and feminist Marxism have been employed to solve the research questions. This framework also helps to highlight the position of women and their class in a given society, the issue of class and gender, ultimately resolving the ambiguity, which often comes to the fore while employing the Marxist theoretical perspective. The chapter also offers the justification for employing Marxism as a theoretical perspective for an anti-Marxism novel, *The God of Small Things*. Similarly, this framework also helps to solve the issues of class and gender in *The Bride*.

Chapter IV:

This chapter presents an in-depth analysis/discussion on both the novels from the perspective of social and political marginalization of female characters through well marked passages sifted from the novels.

Chapter V:

Key findings from the analysis of the data have been discussed in this chapter.

Significance of the study:

As far as the significance of the study is concerned, the study would be beneficial to the readers, from novice scholars to the academicians, as it highlights not only the women's rights but how far a woman is entitled to her rights in multi-cultural societies such as India and Pakistan where various forces of patriarchy, imperialism and globalization are simultaneously in action. At the same time cultural oppression with multifaceted features of religion, class, gender etc. is highlighted. This research work is especially significant in the study of cultural assimilation; in India the assimilation of customs into religions; Christianity into Hinduism and vice versa and in Pakistan cultural assimilation of Muslims previously living with Hindus in the Subcontinent as well as the assimilation of tribal values into Islamic value system which has affected women in general, in attaining an equal status. The novels *The God of Small Things* and *The Bride* are complex texts set in the equally complex societies of India and Pakistan. The research questions raised in the context of women's rights are answered in the political and social context of the said societies.

'All feminist criticism is in some sense revisionist, questioning the adequacy of accepted conceptual structures' (Showalter, 1981, p. 183). Keeping this view in mind the present study intends to probe the 'women question', to borrow the phrase from feminist discourse, that is marginalization of South Asian women from mainstream cultural politics and to uncover the reasons and tentative solutions to this phenomenon. The study on *The God of Small Things* explores the marginalization of

Indian women and *The Bride* of Pakistani women.

Chapter Two

**Literature Review**

As the first chapter introduces the thematic importance of the issue, i.e. marginalization of South Asian women in the context of *The God of Small Things* and *The Bride*, research in this area of study abounds. The novels have been studied extensively from the said perspective. Following is the review of the literature, books, journal articles as well as scholarly works undertaken previously:

Gender role or gender relations, as observed by Agarwal (1996), refer to the relations of power between women and men, manifested in a variety of practices prevalent in the society; ideas;

representation in the society such as gender roles, ascribing some tasks to women pertaining to their weak physical strength, and ascribing some to men for their strength; division of labour; distribution of resources between men and women and attributing different attitudes, desires, personalities and patterns of behavior to them. Gender relations are also constituted by the practices and ideologies with other structures of social hierarchy like class, caste and race; therefore, they are socially constructed relations, rather than being biologically motivated and are subject to change with the passage of time and the constraint of space. A misconception related to the gender roles, is the idea that they are only limited to the relation that exist between men and women. In fact, gender roles are not limited to the relations of women and men, they also signify the relations between men and men and women and women, and e.g. how two women under the same roof relate to each other gendered by the household men; the relationship of a woman and daughter-in-law is another striking example in this context.

Gender relations are also characterized by cooperation and conflict, as observed by Agarwal (1996). Their hierarchical character is influenced in a given situation through dealing, i.e. bargaining and contesting among the participants with varying degree of access to economic, social and political resources. This contestation for the rights can be categorized in three ways: form, content and arenas. Firstly, the contestation in form suggests the covert resistance of individuals to overt group mobilization. This resistance in form, is, again, characterized by changing degree of overt individual action to covert resistance in between, which implies that sometimes the degree of resistance might shift from silent resistance of a weak individual to his or her open and strong individual protest; and sometimes group mobilization might take the form of silent resistance, depending upon the nature of circumstances. Secondly, the contestation in content implies the resistance against the social or political rules and practices of different social institutions. And, thirdly, the contestation in arenas implies the space within which the resistance takes place; household, community, marketplace and State. This framework suggests how in a society the inequalities are structured and, subsequently, are subject to change.

While studying gender discrimination and solving the question as to whether gender gap is organic or socially constructed, Showalter (1981) found biological theory of difference between men and women as contentious, for biologically women are not inferior to men. The theory of innate difference rests on the earlier biologists' and anthropologists' belief that women are different due to their physiological difference to men, e.g. frontal lobes of women are smaller than men; hence suggesting that the female are inferior to the male. This contention is rejected by the feminist critics on the ground that a woman is biologically at par with man, no matter, she is sexually different. Sexual difference does not imply that a woman should be discriminated or marginalized. The ultimate answer existed neither in the biological theory nor in linguistic or psychological theory of difference of man and woman, but in the social or cultural theory which in turn, is all encompassing and gives answer in a complete way. Social theory studies men and women in the cultural context of which they are the participants. According to her different hypotheses for women's culture have been introduced from time to time by social scientists, historians and anthropologists to bring forth feminine hierarchical systems and to reach at women's firsthand experience of the culture. They proposed that female consciousness and their experience within the culture must be studied. Although being controversial, the women's culture creates a significant theoretical formulation. Lerner (1975) explained this social experience of women, being sidelined from the mainstream history not on the account of negligence of social historians but because women have, themselves, taken their inferior social status for granted and perceived the world in male-oriented terms. They are absent from the pages of history for the reason that they have been concerned with irrelevant questions from the history. They should locate their presence by analyzing it in a women-oriented approach, and considering women's culture within the culture which is formulated both by the participation of men and women. According to this view-point, history should be viewed from the lens of women and perceptions of the values, they perceive; in other words, women should reject the cultural notion of womanhood formulated by men and instead view themselves through their own consciousness and perception of womanhood within the cultural whole.

By reviewing theoretical formulation of gender difference, one can infer that gender discrimination is the hallmark of any society, whether it is Eastern or Western. Simone de Beauvoir (1949), in the essay *"The Second Sex"* had questioned the rightful status of woman in the world. The dichotomy between men and women has given rise to the conflict between them which naturally resulted only in the winning of men. For, de Beauvoir was curious as to why this conflict could not be won by women. In this regard, i.e. the secondary status of woman, Butler (1986) was highly appreciative of the questions raised by de

Beauvoir. She opined that de Beauvoir's theoretical perspective, i.e. the gendered notion of a woman, being a woman by birth, is incorrect, as rather it is in the society that she becomes a woman, eventually theorizes the difference between sex and gender. Sex is to be understood in terms of female's body while gender is cultural in meaning. At its face value, then, gender is a social phenomenon imposed upon the natural bodies. At the most, the difference only implies the biological and cultural differences of body and role respectively. In other words being a female is different from being a woman.

Pateman (1990) related the implicit gender discrimination to the classist texts of political theorists. She stated that the word 'individual' in most of these texts is an abstract one, as women, women-hood and women's bodies represent the private and represent all that is excluded from the public sphere. Her textual analysis of the classist texts traced the absence of women as citizens. In the classist texts she traced the proposition that in the patriarchal system of masculinity and femininity, women lack the capacity necessary for becoming part of an effective public life; on the other hand, men possess the capacity for citizenship as they have the natural ability to use their reason and subjugate women. Women's political position, according to Pateman (1990), ever since the creation of civil society is nothing more than being marginalized. In fact, the contractors and the writers of social contract and social contract theories[1] had been blind to the 'individual'. According to them, 'men' or 'individual' are born free and are equal to each other. The classic contract theorists argued that natural freedom and equality is the birthright of one sex only. They contracted sexual difference as political difference, the supreme difference between men's natural freedom and women's natural subjugation, except Hobbes. As soon this idea of natural freedom was formulated, Astell (as cited in Pateman, 1990) commented that if all men

[1] Social contract theory is the development of a hypothetical stateless society into a state through social contract, binding its citizens to obey the state; Heywood, 2002.

are born free, then all women are born slaves. Therefore, Pateman (1990) concluded that political theorists had been blind to such contention which arose out of a discriminatory contract. She posed the question as to how this discrimination could be justified when humankind is endowed with reason while equality and freedom are natural attributes of humans. She further suggested that modern world of citizenship derives its contents from Rousseau's contract theory which is already badly suffering from gender discrimination, as the latter's political theory draws upon the difference between manhood and womanhood, where man is master of himself and women are mastered by men.

The irony is that the democratic theorists have not yet confronted the implication of patriarchal constructions of citizenship.

Therefore, they are of little help in solving the problems faced by women. Wallstonecraft (as cited in Pateman, 1990) observed that even democracy restricted choices for women, i.e. within the contemporary patriarchal system and within the constraints of democratic theory, it is considered that as active and complete citizens, both men and women should behave alike; women should be similar to men and women's recognition as women and as citizens, cannot be complied as it is controversial to the very concept of citizenship; these ideas were inherited by the present democratic values. This implies that winning an equal status for women demands a radical change, both, in democratic theory and practice. Pateman (1988) was highly critical of classicist theorists and according to her the multiple layers of discourse, which had been dominating most of the world's thought, should be unfolded once and for all. The sexual contract[2] is the repressed form of contract theory; while making a civil society, theorists hypothesized men's society, excluding women from political spheres. The enduring impact of contract theory, in fact, diminishes the perspective of sexual contract more than

---

[2] Sexual contract is the one-sided contract by men contractors which excluded women as party to the social contract; Pateman, 1988.

ever before, so much so, to marginalize, feminist concerns. She observed that social contract presupposed the sexual contract and that the civil freedom presupposed the patriarchal right. In fact, classist theorists have originated huge problems for women, regarding their inclusion as citizens into the fabric of a civil society. This formulation is questionable as to why these theorists could not incorporate women in the societal structure, as women, in to their 'political' and 'political relations'; a woman, as a woman, should be as equal in a civil society as a man. According to her, this repression on the part of sexual contract is responsible for the right to set the patriarchal society. For womenfolk, social contract is the story of freedom while the sexual contract is that of subjugation. This contract is the very genesis of modern patriarchal culture. Every relation whether it is of the employer or the worker in the capitalist market, or the marital contract between the spouses, is the off shoot of that social contract which became the patriarchal order of most of the Western societies. Therefore sexual difference is the political difference. It is the difference between the freedoms of men, as contactors and subjection of women, as subjects.

Although this discrimination dates back to ancient China, Heywood (2002) stated that they were not highlighted until the publication of Wallstonecraft's essay, "*A*

*Vindication of the Rights of Women*" in 1792. First voices[3] were registered in Europe, with the women's universal movement for suffrage in 1840s and 1850s. This brought forth a more radical movement, in 1960s, called the Women's Liberation Movement. The purpose of such revolutionary thought was to enhance the social role of women and to raise a voice against the sexual and gender inequalities and overturn male domination in the society. Some of the outrageous voices against this discrimination ascribed the patriarchy, being the political and fundamental cleavage in the society, the institution which controls the half of the population, i.e. female. For them

---

[3] The first-wave feminism.

personal subjugation leads to political subjugation and, therefore, reforms in the personal, domestic and family life is to be needed.

It is in this connection that Lerner (1986), claimed that women have always been in the capacity of making history and producing a society but they have been denied the chance or role to perceive and comprehend history in their own way. Women have been intriguingly sidelined from active role in the society; they have been denied theory formation as well. Lerner called this drift of history with the role of the women as 'the dialectics of women's history'[4](p. 5). According to her it

---

[4] To Lerner, dialectic means the historical

is this dialectic, the competing forces, that has been the driving force for women to assert themselves. This propelling force and the present status of women demonstrate a sharp contrast between her creative role and the constraints of marginality in the meaning giving process.

Women's position in a society has been the leading question of feminists because men tend to have a more prestigious position than women, as they remain outside the mainstream culture. Any woman who deviates from the norms of society is a deviant, a manipulator or an exception. According to Ahmad (as cited in Jafri 2008),

---

process whereby women remained unable to interpret their actual historical experience; Lerner, 1986.

patriarchal family arose to control women's reproductive body by men which was sanctioned and codified by the State. As women were designated as the property, they were subjected, at first, to the control of fathers and later on to their husbands and laws and constraints became tighter and tougher for them.

Viewing this perspective, i.e. the gender issues, from global level to local, from the South Asian perspective, it becomes clear that although marginalization is a common phenomenon in all societies, it is an issue more pronounced in South Asian context as these societies have been the part of postcolonial period. In this context Jalal and Bose (1998) provided the historical context of South Asia. For almost twenty years, South Asia has been an important area of study in the world literatures from various angles, e.g. cultural, political, economic and social. Different elements, such as British colonization, the newly emerged subaltern studies, anti colonial resistance movements, gender-caste discrimination in a capitalist as well as globalized scenario, converge to make the region even more highlighted on the world's map. India being the most prominent place in the Subcontinent or South Asia is rich in its past heritage. While tracing the history of Indian civilization, Jalal and Bose (1998) referred to Rabindranath Tagore who proudly boasts of only two people in Indian history who can be considered modernist and even they, too, were drenched in the ancient past. Nehru, being one of them, the most nationalist of Indian leaders feels at home, being the child of India's deep roots of tradition of almost five thousand years old, interrupted only at the British rule. This implies that India is the embodiment of age-long traditions and is enriched with cultural heritage. Such a place with multifarious layers of traditions is difficult to comprehend. This complexity on the part of Indian subcontinent, with British colonizers and European Orientals, influencing the area, on the one hand and modernist as well as traditionalists, on the other, poses the problem of single interpretation of the area. The binary opposition between the center and the regions, the nations and the communes resists the single interpretation. Class and caste are hierarchical in social structure and gender, too, occupies a lower position. In fact, hierarchy is the soul of India's superstructure, and women are at the bottom. Indo Aryian society elevated the status of women only theoretically and considered it inferior in practice denying her the participation in the public affairs. This subordination increased in the Vedic period. The kingdom in Ayodia, as described in Ramayana, is patriarchy. Further, the feature of adaptability and accommodation in the Indian culture, merged various cults and religions into it; Hinduism, Buddhism,

Christianity, and Islam, to mention the prominent ones. But it is a unique feature of Indian history that in spite of accommodating different cults, it retained its traditional unity even in diversity. One noteworthy thing in this context is the feature of accommodation in the religion of Islam, which not only gave a new thought to its followers but retained the traditions and customs of the Arab society. Therefore, when Islam came into the subcontinent, it quickly adapted itself to the Indian culture, which was already hosting the other religions; hence brought forth Indo-Islamic culture in India. The specificity of these cultures, according to Jalal and Bose (1998), is the fact that both Hindu and Muslim women were left out of public domain which, again is the dominant feature of South Asian cultural history.

Marginalization of women, as depicted by Moghadam (2007), is a historical pattern and South Asia is not devoid of it. She observed that Middle Eastern societies, North African and South Asian countries contain demography which is known as the 'patriarchal belt' and are the areas under the siege of political turmoil, cultural conflicts and social change. The region is confronted with various challenges like political and military debates. At the same time the struggle between liberals and traditionalists; feminists and fundamentalists; upholders of equality and of identity and difference, is marching ahead. This has resulted in the emergence of women's movements which are daringly fighting against strict cultural norms and patriarchal gender relations prevalent in the region. These movements are questioning the status quo, while forming alliances to call for the process of democratization, economic empowerment of women and peaceful conflict resolution in the region. These movements are the natural outcome of South Asia's age long patriarchal structure and its implications for the gender relations; with adverse impact on women's status. The impact of globalization, along with the existing patriarchal values, is double fold on the condition of women.

In fact, according to Agarwal (1996), there is little information on gender studies on South Asia, yet some of information collected through sociological and anthropological studies on South Asia, is concerned with marriage and kinship which sheds light on women's position in different communities as to their socio and economic strata; hence ethnographic literature up to 70s presents an ungendered position of women. Women are present in the society only in the capacity of objects of exchange and not as subjects, they appear without any voice of their own, and gender relations do not present any problem. The implied meaning of such description is the idea that women are in a subordinated position, because of their social roles, e.g. of mothers and of wives, etc. and of the culture, of which they are the members.

The fact that the voice of women in South Asia is much more expressive is evident from the reading of its literature, observed by Hussain (2005). Whether the indigenous South Asian women writers, living in Pakistan, India or Bangladesh and Sri Lanka, or living in diaspora, write differently from their male counterparts, especially in delineating their female protagonists in the fiction; they fix their women in the definitions of their own, the liberated women and specially in the emerging concept of 'new women', the radical women, liberating from its traditional stereotyped image. Feminist views of the authors shaped their texts in the light of their culture and they aimed at raising issues which concerned gender in South Asian culture. The placement of women in the specific culture of South Asian history is a dominant political discourse on the part of women writers, e.g. Deshpande, Mehta and Desai, observed Hussain (2005). Historically speaking, this new woman has been the driving force for social change, while struggling for the equal rights in education, economics etc. and who has questioned the very norm of the society. This struggle for identity is in the backdrop of nineteenth and twentieth century feminist movements, first emerged in Europe and seeped into various cultures, including South Asia. The women in South Asia shunned their traditional roles and emerged as creative force to uplift women's lot. Therefore, the same image emerged in the women's writing as an escaping from the constraints of families, questioning the patriarchal concepts of society, such as the cultural norms and oppressions and consequently establishing their place in a male-dominated society. The notable thing about the women portrayed in South Asian literature is that as liberating women they become individuals recognizing their identity; adopt a way to free themselves from the shackles of traditions, disregarding the outcome of the transgression. This selfhood on the part of women is a journey, symbolic and literal, undertaken mentally, psychologically and geographically. This transforming journey compels them to assert their individual beings, negating their traditional roles and merging into the new, changing ones. This is the theme presented by women authors in South Asian literature. The protagonists are the embodiment of self-willed individuality. South Asian protest writing emerged from the traditional submissiveness of women embodied in Hindu goddesses 'Sita' and 'Savitri'. Through the images of Sita and Savitri Indian women were persuaded to follow their way of faithfulness and devotion to the family. Protest writing of South Asian women is the very contrast of these traditional images. In the context of Indian writing the dominant theme is the trapping of women in the familial role, and their exploitation at the hands of culture. According to Hussain (2005), Desai, Saghal, and Markanday projected their dissatisfaction with the roles of women in the society. Two kinds of women, conformist and non conformist are presented in the Indian writing, the former catering to the desires of men and letting themselves to be subjugated and the later transgressing the notions of tradition and culture. Yet, both suffer; One for complying the norms of patriarchy and the other for being untraditional and revolutionary.

Sinha (2008) observed that the image of women in South Asian novels changed tremendously during past few years. The image of Sita Savitri has been the part of South Asian fiction because of some strange pleasure and self purifying effect of suffering and endurance. But influenced by the European Feminism a new woman appeared who stood for her individuality. The suffering women of Markandaya and Mahadevan disappeared from the women's writing and a radical woman emerged. Women in the works of Sara Suleri, Anita Desai, Chitra Fernando, Anees Jung, Arundhati Roy, Bapsi Sidwa and Taslima Nasreen are the subversive images of traditional women in South Asian perspective. South Asian fiction, according to Sinha (2008) is expressive of the dominant discourse by women. It is in this context that South Asian women's writing is the representation of gendered women and their equal place in the society.

*South Asian Novelist in English: An A-Z Guide*, edited by Sanga (2003) depicted Sidwa's novel, *The Bride* as celebrating the theme of liberty which she highlights in the Pakistani context. Her novel comprehensively views the women belonging to the subcontinent and their common problems. The woman in this society is considered as belonging to the animal lot. *The Bride* is a commentary on the value system of tribal people, their way of living and above all their code of honor in their patriarchal system.

In his book *Bapsi Sidwa,* Singh (2005) explained *The Pakistani Bride* as the story of patriarchal society of Pakistan. According to him, the crux of the novel highlights the suffering of women in the patriarchal society where they are inhumanly treated. They have to attend the needs of the men. The norm of respecting the women is beyond comprehension as men do not falter to beat their old mothers, let alone their wives.

Nelson (2000), in his book *Asian American Novelists: A Biographical Critical Sourcebook*, wrote that Sidwa as a Westernized woman is criticizing the traditional patriarchy, and the way South Asian women's lives are controlled by their fathers, husbands and sons. Her novels, especially *The Bride* has the underpinnings of societal evils including the patriarchal oppression and the Hadood Ordinance of the then Zia's military cum Islamic regime. At the surface, her novel's appeal as observed by Nelson (2000), might be ascribed to the dominant rule of men and the consequent female oppression but deeply they the critiques of unjust legal and political system of the dictatorial rule (Nelson, 2000).

Dodiya (2006), in *Parsi English Novel*, related Sidwa's experience of living in Pakistan. For Sidwa, getting close to the tribal society, while staying with her husband at a tribal hilly resort was a horrifying experience, as the real incident of a tribal woman's murder by her husband, who had transgressed the norms of the society, haunted her. The incident reflected the oppressed conditions of women, not only in Pakistan but in the subcontinent. *The Pakistani Bride* is the depiction of inhuman treatment of Pakistani women. When a woman is contracted into marriage to a tribal man, she becomes the inseparable part of that society and transgressing the norms means dishonour to the family which ultimately ends in death. The irony is that the violation of the honour of husband becomes the shame and dishonor for the whole tribe and the whole tribal community takes part to purge the guilt off by killing the woman. The novel highlights the struggle of women against the oppression of patriarchic, tribal culture, where women's victimization is a norm, an unquestioned tradition. Indra Bhatt (as cited in Dodiya, 2006) related this predicament of Pakistani women with their spiritual journey. Zaitoon's painful journey from the plains of Lahore to the tribal Kohistan is the symbolic journey of a woman, from the world of imagination to realities of life, the world where men treat women savagely. This book is valuable as it also comments on the domination of one culture over the other; in this case the domination of tribal over the culture of plains.

In another of her book *Critical Essays on Indian Writing in English*, Dodyia (2006) noted that like all Third World women writers Sidwa challenges the patriarchal oppression of Pakistani society and tries to redefine the power structure where men subjugate women. The society to which Sidwa belongs is the victim of both patriarchal and imperialist oppressive orders, which are complementary to each other; the one, being the same to the other oppression. The fight to subvert the imperialism needs to topple the patriarchy first. Women in the Third World perspective are doubly marginalized, through man, who is their father, husband and son and then through them bound by the 'Imperial' center which is in the form of State. Hence women in the Third World perspective, struggle, to come out of the peripheral zone and challenge the power of center held by men. While commenting on the women's weak position in a colonized world Sidwa (as cited in Dodyia, 2006) expressed that the logic behind the oppression of a men is their frustration of being themselves oppressed at the hands of imperialism. The only expression of men's weak position is the victimization of women. This is the vicious cycle of oppression which goes on unchallenged. Sidwa's analysis of Wallstonecraft's views suggests that European woman is the victim of the Industrial Revolution, which was the expression of the oppression of imperial center.

Sidwa is critical of some of the features of Pakistani culture and society, as observed by Brains (2003), in *Modern South Asian literature in English*. Telling the story of a ten year old Qasim who is married to a girl, five years older than him, Sidwa, as observed by Brains (2003) interweaves a multiple layered story, stretching from his married life to his migration to the city after his family's annihilation in the epidemic of smallpox, to the Partition and his settling in Lahore with his adapted child Zaitoon. It is the life of Zaitoon that is the focus of Sidwa's critique. While living in the open culture of Lahore, she has been committed to a tribal man for marriage by her father. Outwardly, Qasim, being the part of the tribal roots of his traditional culture, pledges his daughter to a forced marriage but implicitly he is relieving himself of the responsibilities of a father, as a woman in South Asian culture is a burden on her parents and marrying a woman to a tribal means receiving a bride's price. Sidwa highlights the insensitivity on the part of the traditional culture, where fathers and husband are ignorant of a woman's consent in a marriage. *The Bride* is the portrayal of Pakistani culture (and language) and a message to the foreign audience.

Although for Sidwa's women characters, the struggle for equality may not be the part in the larger context of South Asia, their struggle, is about to transform their own society in the context of equal rights for women. The *Fiction of South Asians in North America and the Caribbean: A Critical Study of English-Language Works since 1950* by Wong and Hassan (2004) depicted Zaitoon as a woman who struggles against the ultra orthodox tribal society. Her struggle implies the birth of 'Sita' the goddess, liberating from the shackles of enchained relations and from the culture which demands complete submission of a woman, not only physically but mentally and spiritually. Her own transformation is the realization that a sound relation demands an equal partnership in marriage. Sakhi's controlling, dominating behavior; his use of Zaitoon's body; his jealous behaviour, arisen out of the company which Ashiq gave to them, while on their way to the mountains and his subsequent madness on his wedding night makes Zaitoon to revolt against her customs.

Khan (1995) in her article "Indian Subcontinent: Pakistani Writing in English: 1947- to the present: A Survey" wrote about Sidwa's preoccupation with the women in patriarchal society of Pakistan. Alvi, Baseer and Zahoor (2012), situate *The Bride* in the context of Pakistani patriarchal society where Sidwa's female characters resist the gender based definition of woman by patriarchy. Marwa (2008) studied the novels of Sidwa in the context of pre and post partition era of Subcontinent. Focusing on the imagery which the female bodies in *The Bride* depicts, it was highlighted that the suffering and helplessness of women in the patriarchal society. This exploitation of women's bodies is the price of the system which a Pakistani woman has to pay for being at the receiving end of men's control. The novels *The Bride* and *Cracking India* encompass different women, from rural to tribal, to depict the cultural and social Pakistani milieu. The historical perspective through which Sidwa's novels are written, is intentional on her part as the social environment in Pakistan has changed very little from the setting and the time of the novels.

Ahmad (2013) studies the feminist readings of the novel *The Bride* in the context of the conquered land. Zaitoon is portrayed as the recipient of violence at the hand of her patriarchs. According to him the novel's imagery is captivating for its focus on the portrayal of violence on women's body. The comparison between the woman as a body and the captured land is striking one.

Khan (2013) in her analysis of *The Bride* says that the novel takes the women's issues not only at the local level of Pakistani society but depicts it in universal terms, describing the general subjugated conditions of women prevalent throughout the world. Studying the novel in the context of Pakistani society she relates the Quranic injunction of equality between men and women. She suggests that the persistence of women's plight is due to their ideology, they perceive for themselves. While making a comparative study of Pakistani and South Asian English fiction, Shamsie (2011) relates the commonality between their literatures with the shared regional and colonial history, which have been the prominent feature of these societies. But according to her Pakistani literature is also distinguished for the Muslim ideology. Therefore Pakistani English fiction emerges from the writers who share Muslim Identity as well.

Sanga (2003) depicted *The God of Small Things* as the narrative of middle class Syrian Christian Kerala community living in strange paradoxes, the feature of the novel which rarely captures the reader's eye. While deeply enrooted in India's traditional society it feels itself to be the part of Western culture at the same time. The novel delineates the hurting and extremely painful social history of Christians of Kerala and Roy being Syrian Christian herself, exposes this consciousness, of up rootedness from the Christian traditions, implanted into the deeply traditional soil of Indian culture, yet maintaining Christian's values at the same time. While depicting their beings, being torn between the opposites, she brushes the picture of the community with sympathy and irony at the same time.

*The God of Small Things* focuses on the individual lives of women characters in the novel, Rahel, from whose point of view, the story is unfolded; Mammachi, the elderly lady of the house, Ammu, her daughter; Baby Kochamma and the cook Kochu Maria, all present different lives. It is in the light of these characters that Roy sheds spotlights on the history of Indian women and the cultural oppression; in the form of class, religion, caste and gender, which has been imposed upon them. This study is carried out by Mullaney (2002) in

*Arundhati Roy's The God of Small Things: A Readers' Guide.* Roy's *The God of Small Things* has been written in the backdrop of misrepresentation of Phoolan Devi[5] in Indian media. Devi's struggle's has much to do to shape the milieu and the female characters in *The God of Small Things*. The novel's themes of generational complicity and the subsequent transgression by some of the characters, like Ammu and Velutha, should be read in India's prescribed rules of love and hate concerning caste and religion. This suppression is again colored by the 'subaltern's muted presence, the feature of

---

[5] Phoolan Devi, an Indian, low-caste, bandit queen murdered high-class Hindus out of retaliation of her gang rape by them. This transgression provides the raw material to Roy for *The God of Small Things*; Mullaney, 2002.

India's historical submission of village women, set against the superiority of men. Mullaney related Roy's representation of women with that by Spivak's and sets against the misrepresentation of Indian women portrayed in the picture of Phoolan Devi by the Indian media. Spivak captures the ritual of widow burning in the funeral pyre of her husband and challenges this, as well as the scriptures of elite caste, the Brahmins, and says that such representation of Indian women is the feature of colonial India's imperialism and the patriarchy, the phenomenon in which the subaltern woman is doubly caught. This 'Third World Women' perspective as observed by Mullaney (2002) is further highlighted in

Roy's *The God of Small Things* where the lives of female characters form homogeneity in the form of cultural oppression as well as heterogeneity in the form of different options of accommodation and resistance in individual lives. It is the issues of marginalization of women from the centers of patriarchy, imperialism and globalization that makes Mullaney's work valuable and insightful.

*Arundhati's Roy's The God of Small Things: A Critical Appraisal*, edited by Prasad (2004), ascribed patriarchy to be the cause of protagonists' tragedy. Velutha and Ammu are punished by patriarchy for treading against the path of tradition. Velutha, consequently, confronts the age long history and traditions. The novel shows patriarchal oppression against the class and caste structure, where men subjugate women, the haves rule over the haves not, the strong dominate over the weak and high caste act as gods of the dalits. History is very much pronounced in the novel as it highlights patriarchal ideology (Prasad, 2004).

The novel is difficult to categorize as it captures different shades and meanings of Indian society observed Tickell (2007). But, historical perspective, i.e., Indian history, its traditions and values is a dominant note in this study. The oppression of women is the central issue in the novel; Ammu's tragedy; victimization of

Mammachi at the hands of Pappachi; and Kochamma's insult by Nexalites, etc, all show female oppression. In fact, Roy, as observed by Tickell (2007) captures this differing violence or oppression and ascribes it to the history. Although Roy defined her novel as about biology and transgression, later she revised it and located its significance in the power and the powerlessness and the vicious confrontation goes on in the continuum of history. This is already implicit in the weight of traditions which is hinted at the several points in the novel. It is in this light that the burden of history gets revealed in the present, which is ultimately connected with structures of power. The laws of love in the novel and the extent of how much and to whom, is set in the historical context of Indian history, like Hindu legal prescriptions on inter caste mingling. It is history which drives the conventions of separatism to get their stronghold at a certain place, in our context the Indian history; it also welcomes the new cults as Syrian Christianity and Marxism. The irony of Indian history is that no matter how much it is accommodating and self absorbing, it makes this system merge into the orthodoxy of the hosting land. Once the Syrian Christians entered the South Asia they became the part and parcel of its value system. The novel also highlights the history of subaltern women and their exploitation at the hands of patriarchy and colonialism collectively. This work by Tickell (2007) is highly valuable for the study of cultural assimilation in the Indian society.

Mishra (2006) in her book *Critical Responses to Feminism* was of the same view. According to her, for Roy, the novel is more about human biology than human history. But Mishra is of the view that a piece of art or fiction is not only a story of an individual writer but it also depicts the story of a nation, of a society and depicts the way in which that same society influences people's lives. Viewed in this perspective, *The God of Small Things* is the story of a society containing all the essentials, like history, religion, economics, nation, class and caste systems. It is in this perspective that Mishra (2006) referred to Bianca's article, 'No Footprints in Sand' in which the writer is of the opinion that Roy not only focuses on the aftermath of British colonialism in the post independent India, she also highlights the converging influences of patriarchy, religion, Marxism and various cultural legacies in the Indian society which are all responsible for discrimination in the society. Denial of the selfhood or identity to the individuals is to be studied in the context of social exploitation on the part of various aforesaid social fabrics. Identities concerning different individuals have been subverted because of genetic reasons, e.g. the hybrid twins, from cross-cultural marriage of Syrian Christian mother, Ammu and Hindu Bengali father, and the other geographical, political, and cultural constraints. The intrusion of the world which Roy hints at, is the exploitative systems of the society and which can be interpreted implicitly in a comprehensive term, 'history'.

Roy is critical of the discrimination of women in the novel; different treatment of daughter and son, Ammu and Chacku. Ammu is severely punished for an inter-community marriage and bringing dishonor to the family, as observed by Roy (2004) in his book, *The God of Small Things: A Novel of Social Commitment.* According to him this work is the work of social reality, focusing on the marginalizing of women, from girls' education, to their marriages, divorces, inheritance or their access to the economic rights. Taking a quick view on the legislation in favour of women including the legislation for inheritance and property rights which has been the part of social reform in India, he read the novel as a product of social problems faced by the women in India.

The book *Indian Women Novelist in English* edited by Pandey (2001) defined *The God of Small Things* in terms of the margins in the Indian society which are in the context of its traditions; which in the modern era still remain unquestioned. The Love Laws in the Indian society got their validation thousands years ago. Roy, according to Pandey (2001) raises her voice against these age-long traditions and taboos. Ammu is the true representative of female oppression at her father's, husband's and brother's hands along with the oppression carried out by female characters in the novel.

Marginalization of women is seen through another lens by Al Qauderi and Saful Islam (2011). They relate the struggle of Ammu at the post-colonial period inheriting the pre-colonial traditions, as well as her place set by Roy, opposite to her brother Chacko with struggle and the encounter of India with the Western countries at the neo-colonial political scenario; correlating the local to the global;

with local injustices encountering the global injustices. So the protagonist female characters question the age long traditions of pre as well as postcolonial India.

Fahimeh (2013) places *The God of Small Things* in the context of culture and politics in the Indian society. She studies the novel through the lens of historical oppression in independent India, carrying the colonial history, the heritage of traditions as well as the neo-colonialism in the form of globalization. Centering Velutha and Ammu, this work studies the novel in the perspective of class conflict. The social position or agency of female characters is devalued under strict caste and class regulation.

While conducting historical research on Indian English literature in the context of *The God of Small things*, Tiwary and Chandra (2009) observed that Indian English literature has the credit to disentangle the history from dominant culture in to the subculture. This literature also highlights the power of the stronger, subjugating the weaker ones. *The God of Small Things* covers the history from the British colonialist period up to the present. Various characters have been placed in the Kerala's social and political context where social sanctions are regarded high. The social structure with all its essential layers is embedded in the patriarchal values. All female characters are subjected to the patriarchy.

Giles (2011) studies the novel in its historical context tracing the history of oppression from India's ancient past. In this historical oppression, India's local superstructure, the class and caste system, religion and the patriarchal forces as well as cosmopolitan prejudices existing within the systems like communism, pre and post colonial oppression take part to marginalize the characters. All these forces converge into the oppressions of traditions, value system and it is represented through all the characters.

Nanda (2012) studies the novel from the perspective of the oppression of women.

According to her Roy presents her female characters as above average in their capabilities but the irony is that all her characters are oppressed in a tradition-bound system of India. Her characters are not easily submitting to the traditions. Therefore in their struggle for their individuality they are at the nexus of values and traditions and the modernity which compels them to revolt against their traditions. The protagonist Ammu is marginalized by her brother Chacko for making her deprived in all respects.

Thormann (2003), while analyzing *The God of Small Things* in the terms of signifier and the signified viewed the characters in the context of dominant cultural discourse. According to the writer the dominating forces in a society establish the rules of unification and identification and influence the already established order, in other words, mingling with the existing system and making a new social order of oppression in a society. In the global economy the social relationships form the exchanges which in turn are reinforced by the Love Laws; of who should exchange what, implying the economic and social forces of domination as mentioned by Roy. This novel, according to Thormann (2003) is a way to resist the laws of exchange.

Patchey (2007) in her article studied *The God of Small Things* in historical perspective where the history travels from personal to political and switches again from political to personal, creating a delusion as to which aspect of Indian history is dominant, whether personal or political; silencing the voices from the lower strata of society. The connection of the small with the big things in the novel, in fact, connotes to the personal and the political. The leaks of Mammachi's pickled bottles can metaphorically be interpreted in term of history's secret violence leashed on all weak characters either by Mammachi or by Baby Kochamma or Chacko which discloses itself in the form of resistance on the part of the weaker.

Marginalization of Ammu and her children is a dominant theme of *The God of*

*Small Things*, as observed by Needham (2006). According to her study of the novel this game of the center and the margin has already existed in the Ipe family, yet this marginality gets more pronounced at the coming of Sophie Mol and her mother Margaret Kochamma. Needham also related the small voices of those women who had participated in Telangana movement but remained unheard in the history of India. Thus she places the history of the novel in the backdrop of women's struggle for equality.

From the above review one thing is clear that social milieu or context of both the novels is the South Asian society and any commentary on the marginalization of women would be scanty if not viewed in the contextual analysis of the text. While providing the historical perspective of the position of women in the Indian society, in his book *A Social History of Early India* Chattopadyya, (2009) observed that the position of women in Indian society is subordinate to men and they are mostly seen as the image of domestic women only relative to the higher position of men as in the dharmastric framework they can only be the wives, mothers, sisters or a widows. The ultimate respect for a woman could be in the domestic dharma. So gender discrimination was an important feature of Indian society and even Buddhism and Jainism encouraged this discrimination.

It is in this context that Abbas and Idris (2011) state in their book *Honour, Violence, Women and Islam* that women in South Asian communities are controlled by men. According to them this lower status and fragile position of women has culminated into the crimes of honour killing during past few years as a number of such incidences has been recorded by the police. The act of violence are perpetrated against those women who transgress the line drawn by culture and religion, especially the line of sexual purity as female chastity is considered more intact than of men's. The honour related violence may include any punishment that comes in the category of criminal damage, bodily injury or death. The pattern of honour related violence is similar whether it is inflicted in Eastern or in a Western society. The book is highly readable as it covers the topic of honour related violence in the context of socio-legal perspective on women and Islam. In South Asian context this domestic violence needs to be addressed urgently as these communities seldom recognize the presence of maltreatment to their women, as the community urges its women to remain silent and patient and any woman leaving her abusive partner feels extraneous pressure from its peers; consequently the women are dubbed as the transgressors or outcasts of the society, so this transgression has multiple implications such as living the life in new way. The life becomes even more miserable if the woman has children from her ex-husband. This phenomenon is explained as the protection of patriarchies. The implied meaning of the argument is that Islam enjoins equal rights for women but it was the seepage of various South Asian traditions that affected the true teachings of Islam. This book provides the contextual information on South Asia and the position of women in South Asian communities and highlights the forces of patriarchal culture dominating women in all fabrics of the society.

The book *Women and Human Rights* by Gonsalves (2011) covers the aspects of women's rights in India as to how far women's rights are recognized in India and what is the effect of legislation and its implementation. According to the author Indian judicial system is discriminatory towards women, and directly or indirectly supports the traditions of which it is the part, although the judiciary stands as the symbol of equality for all, irrespective of the privileged or the unprivileged. Law, as observes Gonsalves (2011), has the capacity to adapt itself to the changes of time, yet the judgments pronounced by it are drenched in traditional images of women. Position of women in Indian society, which is already lower, is represented in the judgments. A huge amount of the pending cases related to women's issues like dowry, inheritance, sexual abuse etc do not fall in the category of equality and they are interpreted in narrow definitions. Since independence India has enacted several laws in favour of women like Hindu Marriage Act 1955, Hindu Succession Act 1956 etc, yet the State is unable to remove those laws where cultural traditions are more abiding than the State laws. Reforming the traditions and adapting them to improve the lot of women is even more difficult as the culture is the all in all in deciding the fate of women. It is also notable that different religious communities are allowed to govern its people according to its own laws and traditions.

As far Pakistan is concerned, the situation is much the same. It is a patriarchal society which is home to different social and cultural environment. The society consists of three classes, like urban, rural and the tribal society. Tribal communities have their own laws to govern through jirga system. In such a division women's lot is miserable, observed Patel (2010), in her book, *Gender Equality and Women's Empowerment in Pakistan*.

The above review presents an overview of the research undertaken previously. The thing which is very much pronounced in the above review is the presence of patriarchal forces, cultural oppression or the other centers as the causes of marginalization of women in the said novels. Yet, what is largely missing in the previous study is the contextual analysis of the novels; the South Asian context. It is the social structure of South Asia which, according to the researcher is responsible for the margins made for the women. The various centers, not only of patriarchy, with all of its institutions, but the other centers, such as imperialism, colonialism or neo-colonialism, are also responsible for marginality of women.

The present study highlights the marginalization of women not only from the perspective of little access to the resources but how far this access has been denied to women in multicultural, postcolonial societies such as Indian and Pakistan. All implications of living in a multicultural, postcolonial society have been studied which directly or indirectly affect women and their access to their rights. This research work is also significant in the study of cultural assimilation which has affected women both in the Indian and Pakistani society. It is this perspective which the present work undertakes and which has largely been ignored in the previous research.

## Chapter Three

## **Research Methodology**

As the present work focuses on the social, political and economic rights of women in the postcolonial societies of India and Pakistan, Marxist theoretical perspective and feminist Marxism have been employed. The Subaltern Marxism has also been incorporated in to the research project to show as to how culture affects the rights of women in postcolonial societies.

I have tried to study the novels, firstly from the perspective of marginalization of women, i.e. why all the female characters are marginalized in the novels under study and secondly why there is a common pattern of marginalization in both novels; the common pattern of marginalization in South Asia and secondly, from the perspective of feminist Marxism; to solve the query as to why Roy is against the communism or Marxism and how far the Marxist theoretical perspective is justified against this backdrop of antagonism against Marxism on the part of Roy's criticism. How can Roy question the rightful status of women while criticizing the very idea of equality among gender and the class and caste in society, which Marxism proposes; in other words, 'Why Roy writes in the way she does?'(Tickell, 2007, p. xiv).

As far the textual analysis is concerned, well marked passages of marginalization of female characters have been highlighted from the texts of the novels, *The God of Small Things* and *The Bride,* through close reading or unit analysis method; marginalization from various perspectives: social, political, religious, legal and economic. In this context, Marxist theoretical perspective has been employed.

The studies which have been taken previously mostly dealt the women question in the subaltern perspective or the agency which has been denied to women in the Cultural Studies. Osslon (2011) studies *The God of Small Things* in the cultural perspective and places women's issues in the subaltern perspective. Likewise Al Qauderi and Saiful Islam (2011) place

Ammu's struggle as a subaltern woman who might have not been able to speak for other subaltern but she made the way for them. What is striking about these works is that both place the women's issues in postcolonial subaltern perspective. The present project, i.e. marginalization of South Asian women in the context of *The God of Small Things* and *The Bride*, locates the women's issues in the framework of Marxism, feminism Marxism and the Subaltern Marxism. What largely is missing in the aforementioned works are the questions as to how Marxism is applicable on the anti-Marxist novel: *The God of Small Things*; how far feminism Marxism is to be drawn upon while women's social position in Marxism is ambiguous. This project solves some of the ambiguities which come across in the reading of the novel which has been set in a postcolonial, multicultural society of India.

To begin with, Roy is anti-globalization, anti-capitalism and anti-Marxism. Sifting Roy out of her antagonism against capitalism and globalization and even of Marxism (on which the present study would build its own critique) itself is difficult. While going through *The God of Small Things* one experiences condensed political, economic and social interpretation of Marxism alongside the anti forces of globalization and capitalism. It is this aspect of Marxism with its multiple interpretations, the economic, social and political, that poses challenges to the reader as well as the researcher to approach the problems in the novel which is anti Marxist in its stand. It is this aspect which is most controversial and most challenging at the same time. In order to solve this problem, I firstly studied the political and philosophical theory of Karl Marx while going through the political and economic interpretation of Marxism and secondly the theory of feminist Marxism, the feminist interpretation of Marxism and eventually employing these theoretical perspectives.

Another theoretical perspective which has also been employed is the subaltern theory proposed by the Marxist

Antonio Gramsci, the Italian Marxist who widened the scope of Marxism. According to him capitalism is not only the expression of economic exploitation but certain political and cultural forces are also responsible for subjugating the weaker classes of the society. This, he called the hegemony of the ideology. For the middle class to fight back the ruling class, the hegemony of the ideas of the bourgeois class must be crushed if class less society is to be dreamed of Heywood (2002). But the problem is that both theories are same in many ways, diverging at certain points. I will justify the choice of choosing the Marxism as proposed by Karl Marx and later on used by the feminist Marxist and only selecting some of the issues raised by Spivak against the oppression of subaltern women and the applicability of her theory of cultural oppression on *The God of Small Things* and *The Bride*. I will also justify as to how economics plays a major role in subjugating women; in other words, justifying the force of economics in superseding all oppression including cultural oppression, as culture is the product of society and society is first and foremost the division of rich and poor, big and small and above all using Karl Marx phrase 'haves and have not'. Whether the society is feudal or agrarian the form of oppression is same, only the face of oppression is changed.

Before building the theoretical perspective of Marxism it is appropriate to start with the analysis of Marx and Engels. According to Marx and Engels (as cited in Axford, Browning, Huggins, Rosalind and Turner, 1997) social history is the history of struggle between the classes in the society, including all the binary opposites, like slaves and free people, master and slave, 'patrician and plebian' or the subjugating and the subjugated seeing eyeball to eye ball and in a continuous fight for taking an upper hand in the mainstream affairs. Marx takes an overview of the history of world affairs and concludes that this binary opposition is present in all the historical epochs, from Middle Ages up to the present world.

According to Marx's theory, the class struggle and its relevant fight for the status quo on the part of the oppressor and resistance on the part of the oppressed is different only at its face value. The oppression remains the same throughout the history Axford et al. (1997). That is why Marx ascribes to the material condition of men to be the determinant of power rather the consciousness. That is the reason, the material consciousness that supersedes culture and the force of the ideas. In other words according to Marx, economics is the basis of the various structures of any society, observed Heywood (2002).

But the problem is that if Karl Marx speaks for the classless society and equal status of the people and if he builds his antthesis of capitalism and speaks for socialism; and in parallel to this line of thought runs Roy's anti-capitalism and anti-globalization, then why is Roy anti-Marxism? As is evident from her criticism of the India society in *The God of Small Things*: 'Their work [the policemen's while beating Velutha], abandoned by God and History, by Marx, by Man, by Woman…lay folded on the floor' (p. 310). While tackling the research problem (how far the economic rights in particular and social, political and religious rights could have determined the rightful status of female characters in the novels under study) this contradiction was resolved, first.

To begin with *The God of Small Things*, Roy is against the role played by the pseudo Marxist, Comrade Pillai whose empty speeches for the caste issues merely showed his complicity for the social structure of Indian society which is divided into watertight compartments. Comrade Pillai and Chacko, the self proclaimed Marxist who could not win the equal status for the untouchables as well as the women in the novel, both exploited the factory workers. Roy intentionally places untouchables and women side by side to highlight social discrimination in the Indian society and the failure of communist party in the Keralite society, as put by Comrade Pillai, 'Change is one thing. Acceptance is another…For you what is a nonsense, for Masses it is something different' (p. 279). In fact as a social or political theory Marxism is a complex theory, as Lenin had described it as the German philosophical thought drawing upon the economic system of the English and on the politics of French political system Axford et al., (1997); this diverse background makes the theory multi-pronged. With this difficulty Marxism has been interpreted in different ways, especially being the anti-thesis of Western capitalism from the period 1917 to 1991. Another difficulty comes from another anti-thesis within the Marxism itself; Marxism as a social and political philosophy and the Communism of Soviet Union, China and other Eastern European countries of the 20th century; both in theory and practice being poles apart, observed Heywood (2002). Marxism is divided into several versions and the other versions such as Naxalities, the revolutionaries backed by China and excluded by Indian Communist Party for their agenda of violent overthrow of feudal, the Communist party to which Velutha is said to belong, is another complexity in the Marxist theory. This explanation makes the researcher to infer the inherent difficulty of Marxism, its various interpretations, economic, social as well as political and its understanding varying from individual to individual.

Having resolved the complexity of the theory, while employing its various interpretations, I conclude that Roy's antagonism against Marxism is not toward the Marxism as proposed by Karl Marx and Engels but the Indian Marxism which has been proposed by Congress Socialists party, in 1934. In fact, as the narrator in the novel, i.e. Rahel, proposes, communism came into the Indian state of Kerala secretly or cleverly, ironically proposing Marxism without questioning the age long caste oppression; a new version of Marxism with Eastern Marxist tilt, carrying tradition bound Hinduism with a touch of democratic values (Tickell, 2007, p. 31). The real flaw with Indian Marxism is that it could never change the plight of the oppressed whether untouchables or the Indian women, the version which Roy is obsessed with, in *The God of Small Things*. As Rahel says, 'It was not entirely his [Pillai's] fault that he lived in a society where a man's death [Comrade Pillai let Velutha, the card holder, Communist Party worker go into the hands of police] could be more profitable than his life had ever been' (p. 281). Tickell (2007) further clarifies the position of Roy while stating her antagonism not against Marxism itself but the flaws of the system which developed in its misinterpretations or during the manipulations of the power holders, carrying the stakes of power in few hands.

While sifting Roy out of the antagonistic complexity of Marxism, the theory of Marxism is paradoxically justified in handling the research problem. Marxism, if not in its pure sense of the term, but in its modified form, is followed it can liberate the oppressed class from the shackles of oppression.

Now the question arises as to whether feminist Marxism is justified in its applicability on *The God of Small Things*; what is the place of women in Marxism or what is the role of gender in society in Marxist perspective? One view among the Marxist critics is that Marx has ignored the position of women in a certain society, observed Bertens (2008), but according him, the position of women can be inferred from the struggle among the social classes. Marxist critics also infer the class of women from their husbands and fathers; the bourgeois women belong to the upper class while the proletarian women belong to middle class, Agarwal (1996). But this categorization according to Agarwal (1996) is debatable as women's class position is changeable with the property status of her father and then later of her husband. This means that through class struggle Marx has implied the independent social position of women. However, taking this explanation into account, feminist Marxists argue for the equal rights for women in the society within its superstructure, the laws, and the economic, political and social systems. Viewing women as a class in its own right, and that too as a downtrodden class, feminist Marxists voice for the equal rights for women.

As discussed earlier, another competing postcolonial theory, the Subaltern theory, is equally applicable on our study, *The God of Small Things* and *The Bride*. Spivak, the theorist of Subaltern theory, voices in favour of the downtrodden people who enjoy no privileges in the society, including women. She rests her arguments on the lack of expression, the voice for equal rights for women as well as the underclass. According to her, women are doubly displaced in the postcolonial age as they suffer from the patriarchal traditions which have been strengthened in the colonial rule and became part of the legal system of postcolonial society: in other word oppression of one age was supplemented by another; traditions were planted on the colonial legacy of oppression Lane, (2006). Although Marxist in its perspective, the Subaltern, as proposed by Gramsci, was redefined by the social historians of India, including all the oppressed class or underclass of South Asia; oppressed not only from economic perspective but also at the superstructures of the society, like culture and social divisions etc., Tickell (2007). While resolving the complexity of Subaltern theory as proposed by Spivak one encounters the double edged problem which arises out of Spivak's own account of the representation of the Subaltern; Spivak defines and redefines the theory in the changing face of the world affairs; Subalternity in the patriarchal traditions of India and the Subalteranity in the globalized world, Tickell (2007). But the problem is that many points in this theory are debatable and conflicting ones as Spivak herself defines and redefines it. And the real issue arises, firstly, when this theory is applied on *The God of Small Things* where the subjects like Velutha and Ammu resist and they have the capability, at least to speak. Ammu speaks for herself when she encounters her brother Chacko several times in the novel as well as the expression on the part of Velutha, whether it is in the forms of gifts to Ammu, or his transgression of making love with Ammu or his encounter with Mammachi at her anger against him, is clearly, a resistance. This example implies that Subalternity as proposed by Spivak, as an another offshoot of Marxism can be drawn on only for limited characters, Mammachi or Kochu Maria, Vaalay Pappen at the most and it is not applicable on all the characters (again this issue for the subaltern's voice is controversial. One view says that the Subaltern has no voice while the other weighs this argument as misrepresenting the concept of Subalternity. It suggests that Spivak implied the organized, recognized voice of the Subaltern as opposed to the voice of the elite, the binary opposition, as suggested by Spivak herself; Ashcroft, Griffith and Tiffin (2001). Secondly, this theory mainly emphasizes the superstructure. My preference for the Marxism has been due to Marx's focus on the class consciousness. Subaltern theory provides the subsequent cultural oppression that is the aftermath of the economic base as proposed by Karl Marx. Thus, as far the research problem, which this study has undertaken to resolve, the access of women to their rights, both theories are drawn upon, incorporating the most relevant points for reference. This is how the issues and the research questions have been structured to fit in the theoretical framework.

It is this theoretical background that provides relevance to another novel under our study, *The Bride*. It is the economic issue at first that needs to be highlighted in the study of *The Bride*. Feminist Marxism is relevant as the novel highlights mainly the economic problems first, as in the case of women belonging to the dancing culture. Again it is the economic exploitation which oppresses the women in the novel than the cultural oppression (This point has been discussed and elaborated in Chapter Four, analysis and discussion, in detail).

Chapter Four

## Results, Analysis and Discussion

As discussed in chapter three (Methodology), marginalization is defined by Ashcroft, Griffiths & Tiffin (2001) as the process of making someone marginalize, to sideline someone to the margin, such as the binary opposition of black and white; of good and evil; or of man and woman, the center and the margin make a binary relationship. But Ashcroft et al. (2001) making a clear distinction between these concepts stated that unlike binarism, the concept of center and the margin overlaps various forces of domination, which can be the forces of imperialism, capitalism, patriarchy or ethnocentrism, marginalizing the weaker forces at the same time. At the surface the concept shows, a strict demarcation of margin from the center but in fact, it should not be confused with mathematical exactness, as unlike the geometrical structures, in the postcolonial discourse, it is confusing to exactly locate the position of the center; for in postcolonial discourse, there is no one center but it is present in many forms of powerful structures, influencing the margins from various directions (2001). Ultimately, the resistance which (resulting between the forces of the center and the margin) the marginal poses, is futile as the center (the center of a binary unit) is replaced by another binary force. In fact, the concept can be defined in terms of power and the powerlessness, the inability of the weaker or the powerless, to have access to the sources of power. The marginality refers to the position where the center is given the privilege of being at the advantageous position as against the sides or the margins; the otherness as imposed by the imperial forces. In postcolonial terms, in fact, marginality circumscribes a number of things, such as class, gender, the structure or hierarchy of power, social and political exclusion of the under-privileged. The fact is that this binary opposition of the center and the margin takes the other binary opposites in its circumference so that the hegemony of one center may replace the other. A multiple circular group of power holders retains the hold on the resources and sets the boundaries and the margins (Ashcroft, Griffiths and Tiffin, 2002).

While commenting on the concept of 'marginalization' Furguson (1990) observed that when it is said marginal, one should ask about the distance the marginality creates, the distance between the center and the margin or in other words marginal to which extent. But this enquiry is problematic because the place or the center from which power is exerted is invisible. When one tries to hold it, it slips away. And the fact is that this abstract, elusive thing has a magnetic power over the social fabrics of a culture. Ardre Lorde (as cited in Furguson, 1990, p.

9) defined it as "white, thin, male, young, heterosexual, Christian and financially secure". Individually these attributes may be less influential but collectively they exert a strong force on its peripheral, urging this peripheral to serve as a security valve for the manipulators of political power, Furguson (1990).

The context of marginalization, as described above, circumscribes the whole scenario of marginalization in the world and fits in the global as well as South Asian (the focus of the present study) perspective, the 'magnetism of historical forces' (Ahsan, 2008, p. 7).

This magnetism of historical forces begins at the very first chapter, 'Paradise

Pickles and Preserves' of *The God of Small Things*. The magnetism of center and the margin gives privilege to male and dominant characters, e.g. Reverend Ipe, Pappachi, Chacko, Comrade Pillai, etc. and makes the female characters, children and low caste, untouchables to get to the margins. A Syrian Christian middle class Keralite family with Mammachi, Pappachi and Baby Kochamma, his elderly sister represents the orthodox Christian values. Chacko and Ammu, Pappachi and Mammachi's children represent second generation and Estha, Rahel and Sophie Mol represent third generation. All female characters in the family are deprived of the privilege which male characters enjoy e.g. access to economic, social and political rights. This access to the resources is further hampered by the constraints which the multi-cultural society of India imposes on the female characters. Ammu is deprived of her rights but her brother Chacko enjoys them, Mammachi suffers at the hands of her husband Pappachi, Baby Kohamma's discriminated treatment by the society is set against the character of Father Mulligan; Baby Kochamma's change of denomination is punished while Father Mulligan's change of religion is hailed by the society, and male factory members enjoy higher wages than the female workers. This contrasting feature runs parallel throughout the text, first at level of Ipe family and later at the societal level to show how women are marginalized against their counterparts.

In fact, the very first chapter takes the readers into the complex social milieu of the novel which has been set in the equally complex Indian context, in the sense of presenting multi-cultural, multi-religious, multi-lingual, and multi-ethnic Indian society. It is the microcosm of the various layers of Indian society. Orthodox Syrian Christian, Ipe family, inheriting a strong Christian, traditional heritage, with Ammu, marrying and divorcing a Hindu Bengali, and loving an untouchable, Velutha; Chacko, marrying an English woman; Paravins, low caste, rice Christians; Baby Kochamma, a Syrian Christian, converted to

Roman Catholic out of love for Father Mulligan, an Irish Catholic. No class of society could escape the eye of Roy. The novel concerns the social hierarchy of Indian society, from Pillai the Marxist, the Orthodox Syrian Christian Ipe family, at the top, to the low caste, Paravins, women and children, at the bottom.

It is this social milieu where values, traditions and the laws, the 'love laws' are the binding forces of '…who should be loved, and how. And how much' (Roy, 1997, p. 31). "They all tampered with the laws that lay down who should be loved and how. And how much. The laws that make grandmothers grandmothers, uncles uncles, mothers mothers, cousins cousins, jam jam, and jelly jelly" (p. 31). And in the backdrop of this 'Pickles and Preserves' factory, the symbol of India's age long traditions, the protagonists transgress, almost everyone, Estha, Rahel, Ammu and Velutha, the Paravin, a low caste, untouchable and Baby Kochamma, (in her limited boundaries and in the age to which she belongs; perhaps a time of transition) daring to convert to Roman Catholic. This identity politics of the 'Who is who?' and 'Which is which?' (p. 2), the legacy of post colonialism, forms the core subject of the novel. The 'usual' question of identity, in the tradition bound Keralite society though seems less significant at the earlier presence of Estha and Rahel in Ayemenem house, the 'Edges,

Borders, Boundaries, Brinks and Limits' (p. 3), the very hints of marginalization appear to grip the lives of the protagonists. The answer of Who is who? and Which is which? probably lies, in Rahel's view, not only in the 'classification' between jam jam and jelly jelly which is the obsession of Ipe family but in the politics of classification, demarcation, marginalization, which is the intrinsic part of Indian culture and society, for 'to Rahel it seemed as though this difficulty that their family had with classification ran much deeper than the jam jelly question' (p. 31). The depth which the narrator of the novel is indicating, in fact, is the burden of history which is ever looming on the value system of Indian society.

Historically speaking, in fact, according to the narrator, this identity politics started not at the single incident of Sophie Mol's death, not at the miserable death of Velutha, not at the transgression of Ammu, not even at marrying a Hindu Bengali and bearing 'a rare breed of Siamese twins', divorcing him and making secret love with Velutha, not at the 'Necessary Politics' of Comrade Pillai, the pseudo Marxist, not at the tactics of Baby Kochamma or Mammachi but long before the appearance of Marxists in the Indian continent, long before the British with their imperialist agenda occupied the Malabar, long before Christian missionaries seeped into Kerala, long before the Syrian Christians got entangled with the Roman

Catholics, above all the remote time of history when the love laws were written of 'who should be loved and how. And how much' (p. 31). In a single account, Roy captures thousand years of history of the continent of India. She observes:

> ...it could be argued that it actually began thousands of years ago. Long before the Marxist came. Before the British took the Malabar, before the Dutch Ascendancy, before Vasco da Gama arrived, before the Zamorin's conquest of Calicut. Before three purple robed Syrian Bishops murdered by the Portuguese were found floating in the sea...It could be argued that it began long before

> Christianity arrived in a boat and seeped into Kerala like a tea from a teabag. [...] That it really began in the days when the Love Laws were made. The laws that lay down who should be loved, and how. And how much. (p. 33)

This is the root cause of 'classification' which lies deep in the Indian society, not only the classification of jams, jellies and pickles (of Mammachi's pickle factory) but of all the fabrics of this society. Ironically but interestingly, in this Hindu dominated society with several other centers of power, the imperialist or the patriarchal forces, no dominant Hindu suffers, no dominant Christian suffers, no dominant Marxist suffers. Those who suffer are at the margins of their respective centers. In a single account, Roy captures the historical oppression, which the Indian society is suffering for centuries. As Tickell (2007) observed that the love laws mentioned by Roy can be traced to the Hindu legal text codified by their sage Manu, the *Manusmitri,* which distinguishes between the *shudras* and the untouchables and sanctions the distinction for the first time. Yet if we go into still earlier history of the Indus valley, even before the coming of the Aryians, Indus had been in the influence of priesthood, the 'priests of the prehistory' as (Ahsan, 2008, p. 29) put it. For, according to him, it was the clergy and not the ruler that ruled the Indus; dogma, doctrine, stagnation and the fear replaced the king, the religion and the progress; when the surplus value of the production was handed over to the feudalist by the fear of God's vengeance indoctrinated into the producers or the serfs by the feudalist. It is here that the first signs of classification began, the powerful and the powerless, the privileged and the unprivileged, and finally the loved ones and the loveless. This cycle of subjugation continued till Aryans brought the idea of the class to make the work done conveniently as Ahsan (2008) observed. This argument is further strengthened by Tickell (2007) that the Indian society with its strict class structure had its seeds in the Aryan race, long before the Vedic and pre-Vedic age. The love laws enunciated by the society have deep and lasting effects.

This is the hierarchical order in which women's place is marginal. They have been marginalized in almost every field of life, e.g. from mainstream social, economic, religious, political and cultural politics. They have been deprived of their due rights in all these spheres. All the six female characters, Ammachi, Mammachi, Baby Kochamma, Kochu Maria, Ammu and Rahel share the same lot in one way or the other and all the men, E. John Ipe, Ipe (Pappachi), Chacko, dominate them as the sole patriarchs of the family. Inheriting strong patriarchal values from Syrian

Christian value system, the Ipe family is the symbol of women's subjugation and submission. Complete denial of the self and individuality for women is evident throughout the novel. Roy structures the live-stories of her female characters in such a way that all these characters form coherence, a unity in their social experiences, developing a linear connection in their characters, making a common history, though every woman's suffering differing to another, yet budding from the same root, the historical oppression of women in the Indian society. Tickell (2007, p. 3) defines the novel as the one that 'resist categorization' not only indefinable in terms of a piece of romance, nor a pastoral elegy, nor of tragedy, nor a flash of magical realism, and neither of psychological or social in the strict sense of the term but a plethora of various things at one time. The same is the categorization of female characters of the novel, not definable or easy to categorize but as much diverse in their experiences as the Indian society itself. The women portrayed in the novel share various experiences different from each other, showing various shades and meaning of oppression, suppression and repression,[6] the words widely used in feminist discourse,

---

[6] Oppression can be social, such as economic and cultural domination, as well as
psychological; Bartky, Sandra, 1979. Suppression is conscious control of desires while repression is unconscious; Freud, 1920.

sometimes all inclusive in one character. Ammachi, the oldest woman in the Ipe family (in the oil portrait hanging in the veranda), is the first one in the chronological scheme of the things in the novel, the point where history begins to reveal itself, is conditioned by the society to look at the road as her husband Reverend E. John Ipe wishes because he himself is looking at the road; though she wants to look at the river.

> Reverend Ipe smiled his confident ancestor smile out across the road instead of the river. Aleyooti Ammachi looked more hesitant. As though she would have liked to turn around but couldn't. Perhaps it wasn't easy for her to abandon the

> river. With her eyes she looked in the direction that her husband looked. With her heart she looked away. (p. 30)

The 'confident, ancestor smile' of Reverend Ipe is contrasted with the hesitant look of Ammachi which symbolizes the power or the traditional authority of Reverend Ipe to suppress his wife to direct her what to do and what not to. The hesitancy and the helplessness on the part of Ammachi show that she complies with the commands of her husband. The contrasting imagery of the river and the road and of the eyes and the heart shows that Ammachi is torn between the two opposites, the implied metaphor for the center and the margin.

This is the patriarchal tradition of oppressing women from which Roy takes the start of her novel. Next to the hierarchal order is Baby Kochamma, whose life history is even more miserable as she stands at the crossroads of strict traditions under the siege of liberal values which are popping their head in the post colonially globalized world of India. The age of transition to which she belongs is even harsher to the one which dares to divert from the right path while adheres to the old norms. She dares to convert to Roman Catholicism for the love of Father Mulligan, an Irish monk deputed in Kerala for studying Hindu scriptures. In the conservative society of Kerala[7] she finds

---

[7] Kerala is a community of people professing traditional religions, e.g. Syrian

excuses for meeting him and it is in the garb of discussing theology that she wants to be close to him; for, inwardly she loves him; or to put it in another way, the only concession the society gives her is to discuss ethics or morality than imaging or daring anything else. 'All she ever dared to hope for' (p. 24), is the only concession that her religion, culture and traditions allow. Being in the Indian society she has to retain the image of a sister, a daughter, a wife or the goddess, as chastity is the symbol of a good woman. But she loves him more than any theology. And when her maneuvers bring no fruit and Father Mulligan gets back to Madras; she

---

Christianity, Hinduism, etc. This feature makes the society of Kerala traditional; Agarwal, 1996.

converts to Roman Catholicism against the wishes of her family. The price of her being a stubbornly single-minded person, clinging to her wishes and daring against her values is the punishment she receives in the form of singleness of status, a miserable single woman's status wreaked on her by the society, as when she gets back to Ayemenem without the fulfillment of herself, without the consummation of her love, she loses the opportunity of the proposals which would have been awaiting her had she not converted to Roman Catholicism. Crossing the traditional boundaries of religion, she cripples herself for life, as it was against the Love Laws, prescribed by the society.

Reverend Ipe went to Madras and withdrew his daughter from the convent. She was glad to leave, but insisted that she would not reconvert, and for the rest of her days remained a Roman Catholic. Reverend Ipe realized that his daughter had by now developed a 'reputation' and was unlikely to find a husband. (pp. 25-26)

Baby Kochamma is an example of a single, marginalized woman, who ever lives deprived in the patriarchal social system. And consequently lives a symbolically bitter cucumber's life which time and again ejects bitter froth. The bitterness deep inside the cucumber is her reaction to the ways of the world for her ill-treatment in the life.

> In the old house on the hill, Baby Kochamma sat at the dining table rubbing the thick, frothy bitterness out of an elderly cucumber. [...] With her cucumber hand she touched her new haircut. She left a riveting bitter blob of cucumber froth behind her. (pp. 20-21)

The over ripeness of the old cucumber is the waste of her life which she has suffered while living in the traditional society of India and going against it and the bitterness resulting from such suppressed life is her reaction toward it. Her changed, modern hairstyle while living in the ancient house of

Ipe family is the symbolic repression of her unfulfilled desires in the traditional society of India. The garden which she is nurturing is another way of expressing her repressed anger toward society, as the varieties of flowers, e.g. anthurium, honeymoon and rubrum not only show the brightness of their colour or the repressed desires of Baby Kochamma but their spiked and single leaves also show her repressed anger.

> Their [flowers'] single succulent spathes ranged from shades of mottled black to blood red and glistening orange. Their prominent, stippled spadices always yellow. In the center of Baby Kochamma's garden, surrounded by beds of canna

> and phlox, a marble cherub peed an endless silver arc into a yellow pool in which a single blue lotus bloomed. […] Like a lion tamer she tamed twisting vines and nurtured bristling cacti. (pp. 26-27)

The symbolic 'single' leaves and 'single blue lotus' is her marginalized single woman's status in the Indian society and the 'black, blood red, glistening orange and yellow' colours are the symbolic colours of her aggression against it.

Yet this daring character who converts to Roman Catholicism - when changing one's denomination is considered a handicap - remains a traditional woman as well. Baby Kochamma prefers to remain within the boundaries of traditions. As far her unfulfilled love for Father Mulligan is concerned she knows that crossing the boundaries of chastity might bring dire consequences. What she could do at the most is to let her anger out at the garden, the symbolic society while taming the symbolic vines of sexual repression.

> Baby Kochamma resented Ammu, because she saw her quarrelling with a fate that she, Baby Kochamma herself, felt she had graciously accepted. The fate of wretched Man-less woman…She managed to persuade herself over the years that her unconsummated love for Father Mulligan had been entirely due to

*her* restraint and *her* determination to do the right thing. (p. 45)

In fact, being the transgressor and the traditionalist at the same time is more painful, for the restraint which Roy refers to, implies the control of the society which was directly or indirectly influencing Baby Kochamma and was hard on her to let herself express her love verbally.

Gradual change or development from one generation to another is evident from the character of Mammachi. Ammachi's revolt at her heart and Baby Kochamma's change of her denomination shows the change or the intensity of transgression at each generation. In the chronological scheme of the novel Roy places this character after Ammachi and

Baby Kochamma to show that unlike them she is a working woman; she adapts to the changing needs of the time and runs business but even at such a historical point when change has begun to appear in the world, she is still in the constraints of traditions where patriarchy does not owe her any respect and even at her elderly age she is not spared of the violence which is wreaked on her by her husband. Mammachi is another loop of that chain who in different circumstances presents a different example of a marginalized woman; the victim of domestic violence at her husband's hands; an example of her own right; a working woman; an institution of motherhood; and an established woman. But strangely enough, she is beaten by Pappachi daily at night and the violence increases further as Mammachi progresses on her pickle and jam entrepreneurs. Mammachi is the typical example of the victim of male chauvinism as Pappachi is jealous of her progress in the business.

> Every night he beat her with a brass flower vase. The beatings weren't new. What was new was only the frequency with which they took place. One night Pappachi broke the bow of Mammachi's violin and threw it in the river. (pp. 47-48)

What is special about Mammachi is not the domestic violence wreaked on a woman but how far a working wife (especially in the prime of her age when her husband was getting old; as the narrator of the novel puts it), a woman who is in the stronghold of domestic affairs and independent in her means, is easily vulnerable to violence and the influence of Pappachi is so strong on the House as well as on the neighbouring people that the visitors really thought of Mammachi neglecting the domestic affairs while successfully running her short business, for, 'To a small degree he did succeed in further corroding Ayemenem's view of working wives' (p. 48).

The typical representation of Indian women culminates in one of the central characters of the novel, Ammu, in whom Roy invests the whole history of India. The chemistry of 'unmixable mix' (p. 44), of Ammu, an average Indian woman, amalgamates, ironically, the various social problems challenged by an Indian woman. Perhaps by placing Ammu at the centre of the novel, Roy weaves a whole complicated web of Indian society. All social problems, economic deprivation, lack of legal 'Locust Stand I', social marginalization, political backlash and suppression of religious rights, get mixed in her character. She is a complete picture of India's social, legal and political scenario. She is a Syrian Christian, who marries a Hindu Bengali, breeds 'Half-Hindu Hybrids whom no self respecting Syrian Christian would ever marry' (p. 45). She is a divorcee, with two children to feed to, with no legal or economic rights at home as well as at the societal level. Ammu's complicated case is summed up in Baby Kochamma's (a traditionalist, representing the Indian society) words:

> She subscribed wholeheartedly to the commonly held view that a married daughter had no position in her parents' home. As for a *divorced* daughter - according to Baby Kochamma, she had no position anywhere at all. And as for a *divorced* daughter from a *love* marriage, well, words could not describe Baby Kochamma's outrage. As for a *divorced* daughter from an *intercommunity love* marriage - Baby

Kochamma chose to remain quiveringly silent on the subject. (pp. 45-46)

The above discussion reveals an overview of the inner layers of the marginalization of female characters. Following is the discussion of the marginalization of Pakistani women in *The Bride*.

*The Bride* or *The Pakistani Bride* as dubbed by Indian literati has been set in Pakistani context. The novel concerns various issues; from the partition of Indian continent, the consequent brutality of Hindus, Sikhs and Muslims etc; the dynamics of political power in a postcolonial, post- independence scenario in

Pakistan, featuring big shots of political hierarchy, their secretive maneuvers to win the political game, sidelining their adversaries by harassing or killing them; to the subtle hints at the military culture of Pakistan and the filthy environment of Hira Mandi, in Pakistan. But the dominant theme of the novel as the title itself suggests, is to highlight the problems faced by Pakistani women. The novel presents an overview of Pakistani women, rural as well as urban with special focus on the lives of tribal women.

The intensity of marginalization is even more pronounced in *The Bride* as customs and taboos along with traditions exert their force over the female characters. Afshan, Miriam and Hamida are the women belonging to first generation, complying with the social code of the society, while Zaitoon and Carol belong to second generation, transgressing the norms or the code of social behaviour. At the same, time the female characters from the culture of Hira Mandi,[8] Shenaz's mother, Maharani Sahiba, the organizing agent of the sex business and her daughter (Shanaz), the dancer, comes into the spotlights in the novel.

Afshan is sixteen year old when she is contracted into marriage with Qasim, a ten year old boy to settle the old scores in the

---

[8] Red light district of Lahore, the Shahi Mohalla, where professional women perform music and dance; Saeed Fouzia, 2011.

tribal family. Afshan's father Resham Khan had borrowed some money from Qasim's father and as he was unable to pay the debt he offered his daughter as the compensation for the money.

> The sturdy, middle-aged tribesman knew just how generous the offer was. Any girl - and he had made sure that this one was able-bodied - worth more than the loan due...The boy was still a little young, but the offer was too good to pass up. (Sidwa, pp. 1-2)

The marriage is very strange for her as well as for Qasim because they were still young to learn their customs and traditions; the early marriages in the tribal societies, without taking the consent of the prospecting couple and the marriages to settles the old tribal feuds or clearing the loans. Both are wonder struck as they haven't seen each other before, "Her heart constricted with dismay - she was married to a boy! […] The girl didn't know whether to laugh or to cry…She began to laugh but the tears of disappoint slid down her cheek" (p. 3). But Afshan, complying with the norms, submits. 'Afshan accepted her lot cheerfully. She helped her mother-in-law, chaffed the maize, tended and milked goats and frolicked her way through her chores' (p. 4).

The novel's first chapter, spotting the destiny of Afshan, sets the milieu of Pakistani culture where dominant rule of men decides the fate of women; their lives and even their deaths. Qasim stands as a typical patriarch who is solely governed by the tribal instincts "Each emotion arose spontaneously and without complication, and was reinforced by racial tradition, tribal honour and superstition. Generations had carried it that way in his volatile Kohistani blood" (p. 23).

Women folk from Hira Mandi in Pakistan are marginalized in the same way. The diseased environment in which the ailing women work for their survival is pitiable. To do the sex business for a loaf of bread, to sell one's body is not only disgraceful for them but what is even more miserable is living an unhealthy life in the filthy environment of the red light area of Lahore. The picture of filth and disgust is shown through the eyes of Qasim who happens to visit the place. The contrast of filth and spicy smells are depicted in these words:

> The pungent whiff of urine from black-alleys blends with the spicy smells of Hira Mandi - of glossy green leaves, rose petals and ochre marigolds. Silver braid hems blue dancing skirts; tight satin folds of the churidar pyjama reveal rounded calves; girls shimmer in silk, georgette and tinsel - glittering satin. (p. 52)

This picture of colours and fragrances in the midst of stinking smells, the depiction of silk and georgette and the seemingly healthy bodies, is just an outward, fiend picture of prosperity of the most miserable lot. Following is the real picture of Pakistani society as narrated by Qasim:

> A woman, bells tied to one twisted ankle, was hobbling around in the enclosure. Her short, thick-waisted body jerked grotesquely. Now and again, a man standing with her in the enclosure shouted, *'Naach, pagli*!' - dance, madwoman' - and jabbed her with cane. At this she would raise her arms and her wrist in a grim caricature of dance movements. Her

jaw hung slack in an expressionless face, and sick yellow eyeballs stared unseeing. Qasim was horrified. Would any of these men sleep with her, he wondered? This was nothing human. It was a sick excrescence...The woman continued her monotonous, mechanical spasms, one hip jerking higher, jaws dribbling spittle. There was laughter and Qasim realized they were mocking her. (pp. 53-54)

There is yet another picture of oppressed womanhood in Hira Mandi. Another dancer, daughter of the Madam Shanaz, under the control of pimps, agents in the sex business, who dances at the tunes of money, lavished on her. The more money, the more, the lavishing of her charms.

> She dances on the money beneath her feet and through the money being pitched feverishly at her. In a blur she sees the pehelwan holds a note. 'Why doesn't he throw it?' she wonders, until she notices its value. Salaaming, smiling, she withdraws with it, dancing. Nikka rubbed his palms together and looked around with the air of a Mogul conqueror about to relish the spoils of his victory. (p. 62)

The dancer dances to the utmost limit of nudity to get them (the men) 'fallen on the girl [the dancer herself], tearing, ripping and dismembering her to satisfy their anguish' (p. 65). This is the picture of Pakistani society where women are forced by the pimps to dance to their tunes.

Zaitoon is the woman who is contracted into marriage to Sakhi by her father, Qasim, who fancies her into the charms of tribal life and barters her for few sheep and few hundred rupees. Miriam and Nikka, her well wishers protest on such a cross-cultural marriage in which Zaitoon would be a misfit match for her future husband, Sakhi. They protest by saying that it is 'because that Pathan offered you five hundred rupees - some measly maize and a few goats? Is that why you are selling her like a greedy merchant?' (p. 79). But as

Qasim exercises his decision taking Zaitoon as his daughter, 'But she is *my* daughter!' (p. 79), he becomes her sole patriarch. While declaring that the tribal live by their own rule, calling their own destiny and are as free as the air ones breathe, he says, "'You will see how different it is from the plains. We are not bound by government clerks and police. We live by our own rules - calling our own destiny! We are as free as the air you breathe!'" (p. 85), Qasim forgets that there is no place for a free woman in tribal laws and customs. She is as bound as the animals or slaves. He forgets that 'A wife was a symbol of status, the embodiment of a man's honour and the focus of his role as provider. A valuable commodity indeed and dearly bought' (p. 119). He forgets that there is a little space for a woman of new origins, new culture or new values. His is the clan of people, who are less accommodating and almost hate any outsider, 'Their [the Army's] intrusion hurt his sacred memories, rekindled the Kohistani hatred of all outsiders' (p. 85). And eventually Zaitoon becomes the bride of Sakhi who 'surveyed his diffident bride with mounting excitement. Here was a woman all his own, he thought with proprietorial lust and pride' (p. 139).

Zaitoon becomes the victim of Sakhi's hatred for her. She is treated with savagery on her wedding night. Her pride and honour is tore apart while for no obvious reason. Sakhi happens to be a jealous man. The army officer, Major Mushtaq, promised good future to Zaitoon and her future husband and Ashiq Hussain who escorted them to cross the bridge. This goodwill gesture on the part of the army personnel becomes the blot on Zaitoon's character and her suffering starts from the very first day of her marriage till she escapes from the house. To gratify his sense of honour, to pacify his hatred, Sakhi tears apart her sense of honour and her sense of dignity, '...the corroding jealously of the past few days suddenly surged up in him in a murderous fusion of hate and fever. He tore the ghoongat from her head and holding her arms in a cruel grip he panted inarticulate hatred into her face' (p. 139). From the day onwards Zaitoon realizes the insurmountable will and hatred of her husband. Though appearing to be adjusted to the new environment, she decides finally to get away from this subjugation where she is nothing more than animal.

Hamida, Sakhi's mother is also the victim of violence at her son's hands. She is beaten by him when she meddles between the ox and Sakhi whom Sakhi is savagely beating and gets herself struck heavily. Zaitoon tries to pacify him but she too gets hurt by him. "'I will teach you,' he hissed, 'I will teach you meddling women'.[…] 'You are my woman! I will teach you to obey me'" (p. 149). This violence which is wreaked over the ox, Hamida and Zaitoon together is the symbolic picture of animal representation of women in the patriarchal system. 'Sakhi shouted and fell on the animal, beating it with heavy stick', 'Hamida cowered under the raised stick. The blow caught her shoulder', 'Sakhi struck her [Zaitoon] on her thighs' (pp.148-149). This imagery of violence on the women symbolizes animal status of women. Interestingly the same imagery of violence is seen in the picture of the sick dancing woman when the sex agent 'jabbed her with a cane' instructing her to *'Naach, pagli'* (p. 53). This image of animalistic representation is again emphasized when Carol, American Pakistani wife, is made to feel as 'a cow, a female monkey, a gender opposed to that of the man - charmless, faceless and exploitable' (p. 103). Being another Pakistani bride, Carol, an American married to Farukh, a Pakistani, shares the same plight wrought over the women. Complying with the demands of Farukh she resigns from her job in California as Farukh, being a traditionalist to the core, cannot bear that his future wife should entertain every sort of customer in a super store. Belonging to a value system different to 'Californian liberality' he declares:

> 'I don't like to see you waiting on all kinds of men'. […] He also made it plain that he did not want her to go out with anyone but himself. There

> had been a row when she had gone to a movie with Pam. She had been terribly hurt, but had later decided it was a sign of his deep and unique love. (p. 91)

As a Pakistani woman Carol has to comply with Pakistani norms and traditions while adventuring with Major Mushtaq without being in the notice of her husband she flings away all norms and morality. She secretly makes love with Mushtaq and escapades across the bridge over to the gorge and becomes the focus of a tribal individual.

> The obscene stare stripped her of identity. She was a cow, a female monkey, a gender opposed to that of the man - charmless, faceless and

exploitable. […] 'They made me feel so …inhuman…' (p. 103)

She is the embodiment of those Pakistani brides who struggle to adjust to their

environment, occasionally fighting against the strict values imposed on them by their husbands. But seeing Mushtaq as another patriarch, she feels that substituting him to Farukh would make a little difference to change her fortune; she succumbs to her lot. But when Zaitoon is chased to be hunted by her tribal men, she eventually realizes that living a subjugated life in Pakistan is not that easy.

This Western perspective, present in the form of Carol, views Pakistani society from an American point of view. Carol changes the destiny of her life, being inspired by the strong will of Zaitoon, and decides to go back to the United States. She is curious of the behaviour of men in the Pakistani society. A woman is killed for the supposed or the real infidelity. She shudders at the thought of Major Mushtaq that a man could kill his wife for any reason, "'…women get killed for one reason or the other…imagined insults, family honour, infidelity…' […] 'Chopping off women's noses because of suspected infidelity' […] '… in the Punjab. Here they kill the girl'" (p. 195). Carol is terrified when she realizes that she could also be killed if Farukh suspects her to be infidel or Major Mushtaq if she had been his wife. She asks him: 'Do you think Farukh would kill me?' 'Who knows? I might, if you were my wife' (p. 195). She feels that 'Women the world over, through the ages, asked to be murdered, raped, exploited, enslaved, to get importunately impregnated, beaten up, bullied and disinherited. It was an immutable law of nature' (p. 197). Singh (2005) explained this social phenomenon in the context of patriarchy. Sakhi hits his mother and Zaitoon when they stop him beating the ox. At the outset, the little bride Afshan is married to Qasim, as her father owes a heavy debt to Qasim's father, therefore pledges his daughter to this marriage. This rule of the father is shifted to the rule of husband where she is to submit to her husband's commands. This submission goes on to the next generation when a forced marriage of Zaitoon with Sakhi is arranged by Qasim and his cousin Misri Khan as she is unable to cross her father. This transaction is viewed by a foreigner Pakistani bride, Carol, as a compulsion which Zaitoon has to comply. She perceives that Zaitoon is like a caged bird or animal and the attribute of free will, which a human being is endowed with, has been denied to Zaitoon.

While discussing the marginalization of female characters in the novels under study, *The God of Small Things* and *The*

*Pakistani Bride* it becomes clear that all the female characters are back lashed from the centre, for one reason or the other. Following is the discussion as to how far they have been marginalized. The answer to the question raised by Furguson (1990) earlier in the discussion that one should ask the distance of marginality from the centre lies in the fact that the characters discussed above are marginalized at a fairly large distance in all the fields of social life; from economic deprivation to political and legal standing of women from the mainstream socio-political scenario. An overview of *The God of Small Things* by Tickell (2007) suggested that the rights of women, as far as the politics of gender is concerned are complex to study in the complex culture of India as several perception of gender oppression occur in India including the diverse religious and cultural background and the various movements of rights held by women. From the gender oppression of Mammachi to Ammu and Baby Kochamma, etc., all women are oppressed in the traditional society of India. Tickell (2007) referred to this oppression as refrain in poetry which occurs throughout the novel with different intensity but conveying the same meaning (as a ray of light reflects into seven colours).

The above overview shows how all female characters are marginalized. It leads to the detailed analysis and discussion of the issue from various perspectives: social; legal; political; educational; economic and religious.

To begin with, Mammachi, the elderly woman in the novel has been deprived of education. While living in Vienna with Pappachi she was spotted by her teacher as a woman with exceptional talent for music. Mammachi's access to education is denied because of the social attitude towards female education in the Indian society. This implies the idea of complete dependency of women on their fathers, husbands and sons. This dependency of women on the patriarchal codes facilitated men to make women ignorant and therefore, unable to challenge the gender inequalities. It is in this context that Forbes (1998) observed that the Indian society in the form of the then Indian reformers curtailed the efforts of missionaries schools to spread female education. Historically it was only after 19th and 20th century that the concept of meaningful education for women emerged. Mammachi is the representation of those women who in spite of talent remained ignorant and therefore dependent on the patriarchal codes.

> It was during those few months they spent in Vienna that Mammachi took her first lessons on the violin. The lessons were abruptly discontinued when Mammachi's teacher, Launsky-Tieffenthal, made the

> mistake of telling Pappachi that his wife was exceptionally talented and, in his opinion, potentially concert class. (p. 50)

And later when she started her jam and pickle enterprise, Pappachi again got jealous of her sudden success and in order to oppress her he started to insult her.

> In the evening, when he knew visitors were expected, he would sit on the veranda and sew buttons that weren't missing onto his shirts, to increase the impression that Mammachi neglected him. To some degree he did succeed in further corroding Ayemenem's view of working wives. (p. 48)

In other word, this social and economic oppression implies that the patriarchy in the Indian society wants to make women marginalize and therefore to backlash their access to the resources of power, for access to education and economic independency leads to the resources of power which the Indian patriarchy does not want to share.

It was the oppression of a woman at her husband's hands; there is another side of the picture where a woman is oppressed by her son.

> Up to the time Chacko arrived, the factory had been a small but profitable enterprise. Mammachi just ran it like a large kitchen. Chacko had it registered it as a partnership

and informed Mammachi that she was the sleeping partner. (p. 57)

Ammu, the central character in the novel is the example of marginalization in all respects. Her oppression starts earlier in the novel; as a typical woman in the Indian society, she is deprived of education, as according to Pappachi, a girl does not need a college education.

> Ammu finished her schooling the same year that her father retired from his job in Delhi and moved to Ayemenem. Pappachi insisted that a college education was an unnecessary expanse for a girl, so Ammu had no choice but to leave Delhi and move with them. There

> was very little for a young girl to do in Ayemenem other than to wait for marriage proposals while she helped her mother with the housework. (p. 38)

When Ammu married of her own choice to a Hindu Bengali, a tea planter, she had the idea of escaping from the oppressed environment of Ayemenem where without dowry she was worth nothing. But there was another hell ready for her in the form of oppression by her husband. He tried to exploit her beauty for his survival. Ammu suffered domestic violence at her husband's hands:

> This fell into a pattern. Drunken violence followed by past-drunken

> badgering...When his bouts of violence began to include the children...Ammu left her husband and returned, unwelcomed, to her parents in Ayemenem. To everything that she had fled from only a few years ago. Except that now she had two young children. And no more dreams. (p. 42)

Ammu, a divorcee and a mother of two children is economically deprived, and traditionally having no place at her parents' house is further marginalized as she has brought two children along with her who legally belong to her husband for provision and sustenance:

> ...Baby Kochamma disliked the twins, for she considered them doomed, fatherless waif...She was keen for them to realize that they (like herself) lived on sufferance in the Ayemenem House, their maternal grandmother's house, where they had really no right to be. (p. 45)

This is the atmosphere of Ayemenem house where Ammu is unwelcomed after her divorce, where she and her children are deprived of the love.

> Ammu loved her children (of course), but their wide- eyed vulnerability and their willingness to love people who didn't really love them, exasperated her and sometimes

made her want to hurt them... (p. 43)

Every now and then Ammu is made to realize her position in her parents' house. Baby Kochamma voices the traditionalist view that a married daughter has no place in her parents' house. The same view is shared by Kochu Maria, the cook in the house, when she reprimands the children for making mess in the house or spoiling the furniture. 'Tell your mother to take you to your father's house, there you can break as many bed as you can. These aren't your beds. This isn't *your* house' (p. 83).

Chacko, too, is reluctant to hold the responsibility of the twins and openly declares that they are not his responsibility instead, millstones around his neck, 'Are they my responsibility?' He said that Ammu and Estha and Rahel were millstones around his neck (p. 85). Ammu's economic exploitation is very much obvious from the fact that although being an active worker in the factory her share is as much scanty as any woman can claim of:

> He [Chacko] invested in equipment (canning machines, cauldrons, cookers) and expanded the labor force...Though Ammu did as much work in the factory as Chacko, whenever he was dealing with food inspectors or sanitary engineers, he always referred to it as *my* factory, *my* pineapples, *my* pickle. Legally

this was the case because Ammu as a daughter, had no claim to the property. […] Chacko told Estha and Rahel that Ammu had no Locust Stand I. […] Chacko said 'What's yours is mine and what's mine is also mine'. (p. 57)

After the scandal of 'sex and death' Ammu had to leave Ayemenem house because according to Chacko she had already devastated a lot. 'Little Ammu. […] Who had to pack her bags and leave. Because she had no Locust Stand I. Because Chacko said she had destroyed enough already' (p. 159). "'Get out of my house before I break every bone in your body!' […] *My* house, *my* pineapples, *my* pickle" (p. 225). This recurrent phrase is the sign of women's lack of due rights.

This legal status of women, this Locust Stand I or *locus standi* resonates throughout the novel; Baby Kochamma's 'fear of being dispossessed', (p. 70), the 'no Locust Stand I' of Ammu and again 'no Locust Stand I' for Rahel.

The implied criticism of Roy on Ammu's disgraced, lonely death and the subsequent refusal of the church to bury her has several connotations. Roy intentionally implied it and leaves on the reader to explore the reasons. 'The church refused to bury Ammu. On several counts' (p. 162). The 'several counts' possibly are, firstly, being the woman, then, a Syrian Christian, then, marrying a Hindu, then, divorcing him, and above all making love with Velutha, no matter Touchable or Untouchable Hindu, no matter Touchable or Untouchable Syrian Christian, as according to Roy, Indian society has its own rules of classification. This is perhaps the last nail which the Ayemenem society, a microcosm of Indian society, in the form of religion as an institution, hits on Ammu's coffin. Crossing the boundaries of religion is perhaps the most lasting punishment for Ammu.

Another thing which is implied is another kind of woman, who is often missed by the readers is, a prostitute, a *veshya*. The kind of women in the novel who are identified by the Kottayam police by shaving the hair off their heads to classify and categorize them as being immoral as against those who are moral, pious and religious. The comparison of Ammu with a *veshya* and categorization of her children as *illegitimate* is another way of society to mark a transgressor and the consequent punishment leashed on her. Ammu's fear of being branded as a prostitute haunts her till the time of her death.

> She had woken up at night to escape from a familiar, recurrent dream in which policemen approached her with snicking scissors, wanting to hack off her hair. They did that in the Kottayam to prostitutes whom they'd caught in the bazaar-branded them so

that everybody would know them for what they were. *Veshays*. So that new policemen on the beat would have no trouble identifying whom to harass. Ammu always noticed them in the market, the women with vacant eyes and forcibly shaved heads in the land where long, oiled hair was only for the morally upright. (p. 161)

This comparison of Ammu with a prostitute again runs parallel to Chacko's illicit relation with the women workers in Paradise Pickle factory which Mammachi sanctions as Men's Needs while punishes Ammu for doing the same thing with Velutha. "She was aware of his libertine relationship with the women in the factory, but had ceased to be hurt by them. When Baby Kochamma brought up the subject, Mammachi became tensed and tight lipped. 'He can't help having a Man's Needs'" (p. 168). Mammachi as a representative of Indian society, having the Machiavellian double standard of morality, ironically one for the (king) Chacko and the other one for the (mass)(es), Ammu, favours one over the other. Her moral indifference shows as though a woman can have no Woman's Needs, as though a divorcee needs no rehabilitation, as though she has to live a sexually suppressed life and this moral indifference culminates at her anger towards her daughter: 'Her tolerance of Men's Needs as far as her son was concerned, became the fuel for her unmanageable fury at her daughter' (p. 258). Ammu's fear of her 'madness', the symbolic sexual suppression and of the madness of women (and of men also) which runs in their family has also been set in this sexual suppression of women. 'There was Pathil Ammai, who at the age of sixty five began to take her clothes off and run naked along the river, singing to the fish' (p. 223). Ammu's madness is her sexually suppressed life which she is bound to live on. The imagery of madness of Pathil Ammai's and her escape to the river and the comparison of Ammu at her madness and her escape to the river places this account in the historical perspective, the history of oppression and marginalization of women.

Another perspective of the 'Needs' which is the part of the dominant discourse of *The God of Small Things* is relevant here; in discussing the position of the branded women of India. As far as the sexual suppression of branded women labeled as prostitutes, is concerned, there is another dimension to this view. Forbes (1998), while tracing the history of Indian women stated that the women's occupation, e.g. doing the sex business, has its roots in the British colonization of India. Domestic or household women's employment was replaced by the industrial employment introduced with the coming of colonialists and it were the men who were employed for the industrial works. The needy and unemployed women consequently had to resort to the brothel houses. In fact, the economic insecurity and the poverty compelled these needy women to take refuge in the sex business. Analyzing this economic deprivation as a historical fact, one can infer as to why Roy takes a sympathetic view in her depiction of the branded women, as society takes a single perspective and remains unconcerned to the economic causes, more essential in the study of the behaviors of these women than any of the moral lapse on their part (the sex business in the context of *The Bride* is also to be studied in the aftermath of unemployment of women in colonial period).

Baby Kochamma, like her counterparts in the novel, too, is marginalized from every aspect. She only gets permission to education when her father Reverend Ipe thinks that she has lost her only chance of getting married as changing one's denomination, (she converts from Syrian Christian to Roman Catholic), crossing the boundaries of religion is inacceptable; her father's approval of her education in ornamental gardening is sanctioned only in the backdrop of her loss as a prospecting wife, for he knew that changing one's denomination could mar the future of a woman: "Reverend Ipe realized that his daughter had by now developed a 'reputation' and was unlikely to find a husband. He decided that since she couldn't have a husband there was no harm in having her an education. So he made arrangements for her to attend a course of study at the University of Rochester in America" (p. 26). In fact, Baby Kochamma's lack of education is placed parallel to the education of her brother, Pappachi, who has served as the Royal entomologist, the imperial scientist in India, as women in Indian context do not get that sort of education which can give them the bargaining and contesting power in gender relations to challenge the gender inequalities. Therefore, when she loses the opportunity of getting married, her father decides to send her for higher education in America. The social pressure is also working behind such deprivation as although missionaries had long established the schools, both for boys and girls and Kerala has the higher literacy rate in India yet women have been deprived of the kind of education that can improve their understanding. In the same context the traditional culture in which the Keralites have been living has been nonconductive in female education. This depiction falls clearly in the context of unequal power relations among men and women in Indian society. In economic sphere, too, she is marginalized, as being a daughter she has no right in family property for 'She was keen. .

.to realize that [she] lived on sufferance in the Ayemenem House, their maternal grandmother's house where they [she, like the twins and Ammu] really had no right to be' (p. 45). The same deprivation, the same inaccessibility to the family's resources, the same lack of property rights, makes her relish the left over things in Ayemenem house and that, too, only after everybody died. 'She was wearing a lot of jewellery. Rahel's dead grandmother's jewellery…reassuring herself that it was there and that it was hers' (p. 22).

> Baby Kochamma loved the Ayemenem House and cherished the furniture that she had inherited by outliving everybody else.

Mammachi's violin and violin stand, the Ooty's cupboard, the plastic basket chairs, the Delhi beds, the dressing table from Vienna ...The rosewood dining table that Velutha made. (p. 28)

The notable thing, here is the conversion of Father Mulligan to Hinduism. Later in his life in India, while studying Hinduism he converts to a *Vaishnava*. Roy intentionally places such a comparison, of Baby Kochamma's change of her denomination with Father Mulligan's change of Faith. Indian society is unaccommodating to the change of denomination on the part of a woman and accommodating to the change of Faith (to

Hinduism) of a man. Even the society welcomes him as Father Mulligan is shown as a preacher at the end of the novel, devoutly preaching the Hindu ethics and the widows keenly listening to him. 'Fifteen years ago, Father Mulligan became a *Viashnava.* A devotee of Lord Vishnu. A few years ago he sent a photograph of himself addressing a gathering of middle class Punjabi widows at a spiritual camp' (p. 297). Baby Kochamma's change of denomination to Roman Catholicism and Father Mulligan's change of faith to Hinduism is again the discourse or the message of power and the powerlessness; of domination and subjugation; domination of Indian Hindus and suppression of Syrian

Christians who are in minority in India. Baby Kochamma's change of denomination is implicitly criticized not only by her family members but the society itself as the punishment for crossing the boundaries of religion is the punishment of singleness for her while Father Mulligan's change of faith is welcomed by the Indian society.

The above account runs parallel to the features of Pakistani society which are not different from the Indian society. Same hierarchy of rich and the poor; of dominant and the subjugated; of man and woman, is the part of Pakistani society. In the discourse of power and the powerlessness and in the discourse of center and the margin, Pakistani women are placed at the far edge of the center sharing the common sisterhood with their Indian counterparts. Using the same yardstick for measuring the amount or the extent of marginality of Indian women, one perceives that Pakistani women, too, are at the margins of power discourse. They, too, are marginalized in every field of life, such as economic, social, legal and religious fabrics of a society. Sidwa's vision takes almost all sorts of Pakistani women in one shot. From Afshan, a tribal women, to urban Miriam and Zaitoon and American Pakistani woman, Carol and above all those women who belong to Hira Mandi of Pakistan, a very noticeable feature of Pakistani society. Pakistan, as a multi-cultural, multi-lingual country, ranging from tribal belt of Kohistan to the plains of Punjab and the mountainous Balochistan, is as diverse and multifarious as an Indian society. Culture, traditions, values widely differ in various areas of Pakistan. Therefore, Sidwa views them all in her novel *The Bride*. But, in such diversity the one thing which is common to all cultures is the position of women. The distance or the extent of marginality of women, which is at the far edge of the center is more complex as the magnitude of traditions and customs begin to appear round the circles of the marginalized. The life of a tribal woman differs from the women of plains only in the degree. The women share the same constraints of domination in every field, from the lack of access to education, to the constraints in marriages, and inaccessibility of economic and legal rights. To add further, the constraints of traditions tighten their hold on Pakistani women.

'Marriages were the high points in the life of women' (p. 74). Deprived of basic rights, Afshan is contracted into marriage at sixteen by her father with a boy of ten years in lieu of loan he owes to her husband Qasim's father. The connotation of a commodity is implied at Afshan's getting married, without her consent, with a man whom she doesn't know: 'Are you my husband?' (p. 3). Afshan asks of Qasim at her first encounter with her husband, which has been contracted in lieu of the loan. Although Afshan's part in the novel is limited, the fact is that Afshan's marriage as a commodity, as an exchange, as barter, at the very start of the novel introduces several issues to the fore; usurpation of social rights, legal rights and economic rights of women, not only of a tribal women but of all the female characters in the novel.

Zaitoon, the adopted child of Qasim replaces Afshan. As a girl she only gets the primary schooling as getting higher education is the privilege of the boys. 'He saw to it that Zaitoon attended school for a full five years' (p. 42). But later Miriam as Zaitoon's guardian objects to her further reading and writing as according to her a girl is supposed to bear children and hold domestic affairs.

'Now that she has learned to read the Holy Quran, what will she do with more reading and writing - boil and drink it? She is not going to become a baboo or an officer! No Allah willing, she will get married and have children'. […] '…does Bhai Qasim think he's rearing a boy? He ought to give some thought to her marriage…who'd want an educated …' (p. 42)

So being a girl Zaitoon is deprived of proper education.

Zaitoon steps on her sixteenth year and she is to be married now. Her father decides to marry her in his tribal clan. Zaitoon is contracted into marriage to Sakhi, a relative of Qasim, a marriage contracted by the elders. Ziatoon's marriage becomes the heated subject between her father and her guardians, Miriam and Nikka, as according to them this marriage is being decided in terms of exchange of things and commodities. 'It is because that Pathan offered you five hundred rupees - some measly maize and a few goats? Is that why you are selling her like a greedy merchant…We will buy her!' (p. 79). Zaitoon is symbolized as a commodity, an object and an article of exchange as claimed by Qasim, 'But she is *my* daughter!' (p. 79). Consequently the marriage contracted, fails as Zaitoon is made to suffer at the hands of her husband, a relationship in which wife is no more than a commodity, no more than a servant as Mushtaq comments, 'A wife was a symbol of status, the embodiment of a man's honour…A valuable commodity indeed, and dearly bought' (p. 119).

The recurring expression of 'my' symbolizes the property status of a woman in the novel. Zaitoon travels from 'my daughter' to 'my woman'. Qasim possessed her as his daughter, imposing his decisions on her, Sakhi owned her as a wife with 'proprietorial lust', for '(t)here was a woman all his own' (p. 139).

Zaitoon's marriage with Sakhi has several social, economic, legal and religious connotations. Being a woman she is socially at the margin, economically she is no more than a commodity , a possession, first of her father than of her husband, legally no standing in the society and finally deprived of religious rights which she enjoys as a woman under Islamic law.

Sidwa is especially concerned with another sensitive issue, marginalization of women belonging to Hira Mandi. She deals with this issue in her master piece *Ice-Candy Man* where the central character Aya is made to do the sex business. But Aya's character is the part of immediate post-independence scenario, the aftermath of communalism which had had its effects before and after Partition; as Aya is a Hindu woman and she has to do the sex business under compulsions imposed on her by her husband, the Ice-Candy Man. But the context of such women in *The Bride* is totally different from the context of *The Ice-Candy Man*. The women belonging to Hira Mandi in *The Bride* are the Pakistani Muslim women in the post-Independence time when the dust of communalism has long settled down. The purpose of such a context is to highlight the problems faced by these women, the social and most importantly economic problems. The picture of the unnamed (perhaps Sidwa intends to generalize the lot of diseased women), sick, dancing woman is to highlight her economic problems where she is dancing to earn a few money for her daily subsistence and that too at the cost of her life and health.

Chambers (2011) opines that Sidwa belongs to the generation of writers who wrote between 1970s to 1980s, Zulfikar Ghose and Hanif Kureishi, being the other ones.(Sidwa wrote *The Bride* in 1983). What is common among these writers and the later ones such as Muhammad Hanif, Uzma Aslam Khan and Kamila Shamsie is that their writings emerge from the Pakistani social milieu, in which the opposing forces of hard line Islamization and the liberal version of Islam are ever present. The struggle for Islamizing Pakistan in the name of Islamic Republic of Pakistan, as declared in different constitutions of Pakistan, created confusion among people as the word 'Islam' was highlighted more than the word

'Muslim'. These writers have lived through that period of Islamization of Zia-ul-Haq's regime, when Islam was used for political purposes of the then military state. Seeing Sidwa's both novels *The Ice-Candy Man* and *The Bride* in this perspective, it becomes clear as to why she refers the dancing women and sex business in her works. These novels belong to the aftermath of Independent Pakistan and its agenda of Islamization program. Although the characters of Shahnaz and her mother and the other unnamed, sick, dancing woman fall in the pre-Zia period (as the time of the novel's setting is immediate post independence scenario), the fact is that Sidwa has lived through the first hand experience of Islamization program of Zia-ul-Haq. As according to Jalal (1995) Zia-ul-Haq had hit hard on the already deprived segment of society, i.e. women. Instead of addressing the social and economic problems of women in economically downtrodden society, he further suppressed them through promulgating different sexist laws. The context of Sidwa's novels highlights the suppressing environment in Pakistan and therefore refers to the already degraded status of women, especially the women from the Hira Mandi. Sidwa is especially sensitive to the lot of these socially stigmatized women who have no other economic source except to sell their dignity.

The overview of marginalization of women of the novels, *The God of Small Things* and *The Bride*, as discussed earlier leads to several issues, marginalization of women from social, legal and economic fronts not only at the local fronts but at the cosmopolitan fronts; both as the patriarchal norms and the postcolonial constraints. To this marginalization, Tickell (2007, p. 37) calls as the 'double colonization or double marginalization'. This dual marginalization is evident firstly at the Ayemenem House where Ammu is marginalized by Chacko as well as by Mammachi and at Calcutta, at her husband's house and secondly at the societal level where Mr. Hollick, Thomas Mathew and Ammu's employers tighten the societal constraints on her. In fact, the usurpation of women's economic, legal and social rights fall in the broader category of double marginalization, where forces outside the house exert strong influence on all female characters. The study of the rights of Indian women as well as Keralite Syrian Christian women circumscribes the role of government as well as the state. To begin with Mammachi's economic and property rights, (the Ayemenem House and the pickled factory seemingly belong to Mammachi but the actual hold of the property as well as the factory is in Chacko's hands) one can infer that Mammachi only owns the property and has no actual control over it. Viewing this aspect in historical context and to use Tickell's (2007) analysis of history's absorption of various forces into itself, such as the absorption of Hindu's traditions into the Syrian Christian's value system and traditions in the novel, one can argue that history's dominant order seeped into the less forceful forces like Syrian Christianity and Marxism. In fact, certain Hindu castes like *nayars* living in Kerala, before colonization enjoyed the matrilineal traditions in which property rights were acknowledged for the women. The reason for this acknowledgement of land rights for women had been the relative liberty of women of keeping the household in the absence of their men in the city for a long time as well as their liberty in their liaison relationship with *namboodiri* men and the brought up of the children resulting from such a liaison in the mother's house was a necessary solution. Therefore, the woman (the mother) and her brothers were responsible for the care of these children. The Syrian Christians got influenced by the then dominant traditions of Keralite society and acknowledged the land rights for women. But with the British colonization the older customs were changed and new laws were made in which the matrilineal system diminished and totally washed away up to 1930s, Tickell (2007).

In this context of history's absorption, Agarwal (1996), studied the land rights in South Asia and suggested the importance of property rights in gender equality. She traced the history of matrilineal traditions of the Indian society. According to her before the colonial rule of British, inheritance rights were determined through the indigenous customs in South Asia. The customs were as various and diverse as the class, castes, religion and the family background. In the light of her research she argued that South Asia's three regions, Northeast India, following matrilineal practices, South India, including the Nangudi Vellalars of Tamil Nadu followed the bilateral inheritance and Nayars of Kerala following the matrilineal inheritance and the third one, Sri Lanka followed either matrilineal or bilateral inheritance. Ethnographic studies on South Asia suggest that all other South Asian communities, except mentioned above, are patrilineal in inheritance practices.

In fact, Mammachi owned the Ayemenem House (Baby Kochamma knew that they all lived in Ayemenem House, their grandmother's house where they had no right to be) under such matrilineal practices of inheritance but till the time of Ammu the Syrian Christians had already adapted to the dominant Hindu traditions of patrilineal inheritance practices. And in that context, Ammu, her children and Baby Kochamma had been deprived of their share in the property. The exploration raised by Tickell

(2007, p. xiv) as to 'why Roy writes the way she does?'; the question as to what compels her to write about the hierarchical structure of Indian society, including the pre-colonial and the postcolonial scenario, perhaps culminates in the questions of status of women, set in the cultural context, as not only structurally but in the content also, she places the character of Ammu at the center of the novel; though Tickell (2007) relates cross-caste relation at the center and highlights Mammachi being at the center of the 'scheme of things' and Baby Kochamma, being at the back of the maneuverings, the evil ideas originating in her head. For the Indian history with its diverse culture impresses upon the women, the weak segment of the society. And in this postcolonial scenario as gender relations not only mean the relation of women and men but also the relations of women and women; status of women is further marginalized by the women as well.

The implication of culture including religion, social norms, economic and legal standing, 'Locust stand I' or the *locus standi* is important in the study of the present research work as they are dominant in shaping the lives of all female characters in the novel. The inquiry of Mammachi's sound and secure property status under the matrilineal inheritance practice being settled; Ammu's deprivation under the influence of dominant Hindu inheritance practices needs to be discussed here. Ammu loses her right to property under such assimilation of culture, assimilation of Syrian Christianity in Brahmanism. Describing such cultural context Tickell (2007) referred to the various references of this assimilation of the less dominant to the more dominant order in the novel. The reference of Saint Thomas is used to retain the high status of Syrian Christians and the subsequent submerging of their value system into the Brahmin hierarchal order. Keeping such a high order intact, the Syrian Christians maintained several of the traditions of high caste Hindus, such as the same community marriages, rituals and strict class and caste boundaries etc. It is this struggle between the center and the margin that discourages the share of the power among the powerful and the powerless; the religious, social or governmental institutions on the one hand and the small, local scale in the form of influential people, on the other; dominant at the one side of balance of power and the disadvantaged ones on the other. The Hindu legal documents, which Tickell (2007), in her study of *The God of Small Things*, referred to, in connection to the caste relationship, which has been responsible for shaping the laws of love, too, determine the legal as well as religious status of women in Indian society. Whether it is the force of religion in the society or the force of the social taboos in the form of its institution that are responsible for distributing the shares of power and marking someone as big or small, the thing is that one complements the other; religion as the part of society affects the social behavior; and society, in turn, affects the making and shaping of religion. In this context Lingat (as cited in Agarwal, 1996) observed that *shastras* are important points of reference as they not only drew upon the then Hindu customs but affected the customs in turn (Agarwal, 1996). Ammu's lack of *locus standi*, the Locust Stand I in the novel, is, both the part of religious and social agenda of women's marginalization to which Tickell (2007) referred to as the 'interconnectedness of the world' (Tickell,

2007, p. 11). It is this interconnectedness of religion and society of which Roy is careful enough to communicate, and does so indirectly, as Tickell (2007) opined that Roy's method of communication of her ideas regarding the political and moral judgments is implied.

Ammu's lack of Locust Stand I is a double edged problem; religious as well as societal. Considering the assimilation of cultures mentioned above, Ammu's legal status has been affected by the Hindu traditions of inheritance, which is patrilineal. Hindu legal documents, consisting mainly the legal treatise, *Dharmashastras*, (the same legal document which prescribes the hierarchy of caste system, which, keeping in mind the complex social system of India, places *brahmins* at the top of the hierarchy), as noted by Tickell (2007), describes the inheritance and marriage practices. These *shastras* divided further into two doctrines, *Mitakshra* and *Dayabhaga*, affected legal practice in the colonial period of British, which in turn, influenced the contemporary Hindu laws. Under both laws, property status of women is recognized but in a complex way. The *Mitakshra* doctrine recognizes joint and separate property, allowing inheritance only to male members of the house in the joint property as a man has exclusive control over his separate property, and excluding women as coparceners. Under this system women were only entitled to maintenance, and that too in case of becoming the wife and as daughter who are not married (while in case of marriage of a daughter she is entitled to gifts and marriage expenses) in other words being sidelined from the lion share of the property. In *Dayabhaga* there was a little recognition of widow or a daughter's right. Female property was only recognized in the terms of *stridhan* which means only movable property, (various interpretations on *stridhan* by various schools of thought provides movable property in explicit terms) as observed by Agarwal (1996), such as clothes, small things gifted at the time of her marriage. Ammu's anger at her lack of Locust Stand I, perhaps, is in this context, as she has negligible right over the property of her parents and contracting her marriage herself she loses the already scanty dowry from her parents. A woman's property status being diminished as per rule of patrilineal inheritance practice, another implication of her deprived status might be referred to the marriage practices in certain Indian society. Ammu's lack of Locust Stand I is related to the marriage and inheritance practice in Keralite society. In fact, as mentioned above an average Indian woman is affected both by her own culture or the customs of her own tribe or caste, as well as the dominant culture of India, in this case the culture which Hinduism generated. In a Keralite society, such as among Nayars, of both central and north Kerala, land was traditionally controlled through a joint family system and inheritance was through the female line, observed Agarwal (1996). In Kerala women continued to live in their natal home or villages after their marriage, to be able to maintain control over the property. It is noteworthy that these societies who acknowledge the rights for women also make it conditional that their women contract marriages in the same caste or cross cousin marriages in the same villages so that the landed property might not be lost to a stranger, observed Agarwal (1996). The case of Ammu's loss of property might be referred to her cross-caste marriage, which Baby Kochamma refers to as intercommunity marriage, a marriage to a Hindu Bengali which is far off from her natal village and that too against her parents' wishes, therefore when 'She wrote to her parents, informing to her decision. They didn't reply' (p. 39). Another thing which is also noticeable in this context is the reference in the novel, of the practice of inbreeding among Syrian Christians. It testifies to the fact that the Ipe family adapted to the traditions of the then dominant society of Nayars of Kerala. This transgression on the part of Ammu and Chacko of marrying outside their community make Ammu to lose her chance of landed property which her mother Mammachi had inherited in matrilineal inheritance practice. 'Chacko said that Estha and Rahel were indecently healthy. So is Sophie Mol. He said that it was because they didn't suffer from Inbreeding like most Syrian Christians. And Parsees' (p. 61). Another pattern to the disinheritance of women is traceable by the fact that matrilineal and bilateral system of inheritance favoured the women for getting social and economic security. These traditions could not get hold on in the changing times of legal and economic changes when colonial and postcolonial forces were emerging in the Indian society. The large pieces of land got partitioned and divided; the egalitarian system of land changed into different economic system; the forces from the capitalist market seeped into the lives of the people; means of productions as well as the gender roles changed and the patriarchal rule popped its head and the women suffered tremendously under the effects of new changes, observed Agarwal (1996); with the market invasion the things changed swiftly. During the British rule the marriage and inheritance practices, land rights of the daughters, marital residence, and widow and divorcee remarriages all changed and affected women directly and indirectly. English Victorian morality, prescribing strict rules in relations, restricted the freedom of women which they enjoyed under matrilineal system. The younger generation educated in the metropolis of

Madras and abroad especially England, affected by cross-cultural values such as the absorption of Tamil-Kerala-Brahminical and European ideas, began to look down upon these practices of marriages and sexual liberty, their mothers and sisters enjoyed earlier (Agarwal, 1996). This situation of marginalization of women is also analyzed by Tickell (2007) in the same context when English colonials passed the strict discriminatory laws against women. It is in these changing circumstances that Ammu not only loses her Locust Stand I but becomes the victim of cross-cultural forces which all have been active in marginalizing the women. The various forces of Syrian Christians; Keralites; of Hinduism; of

Victorian moral standards and the British colonial forces with its own colonial laws tightened the liberty of women and the multi-pronged rule of men, capitalism, patrilineal laws and the patriarchy began to influence the women in Indian society.

This is the context of India where Roy sets her novel. Under the cross-cultural influences, the authority transfers silently from Mammachi, a woman of independent means, managing large fields and owning a factory, to Chacko, the patriarch who makes Mammachi the sleeping partner of her own enterprise and excludes Ammu not only from the share in the factory but also from the Ayemenem House when he learns about her sexual relation with Valutha. This cultural fusion of Victorian morality and of the piety of Hinduism as well as the forces of Syrian Christianity compels Chacko to make Ammu leave the house. 'Get out my house before I break every bone in your body!' (p. 225). It is the breach of honour, the breach of Victorian morality and the breach of the authority of Syrian Christian church to expel its members from the church that Mammachi scares when she is informed by Vallay Pappan that Ammu had been to the beach with Velutha for several times and that makes Ammu to leave the house, observed Tickell (2007). It is 'intermixture or cross- cultural fertilization of South Asian contemporary cultures' as put by Tickell (2007, p. 5) that makes Ammu to go away. It is the force of patriarchy, in the form of dominant religious and cultural forces that makes Chacko, the patriarch of the house and of the society at large, so strong to impose his decisions on her sister and mother, and ironically so strong to break the same rules for him, himself.

Seeing the marginalization of women and the usurpation of their rights at the social and political context as Tickell (2007) analyzed, one perceives that social and political issues do have commonalities; the dictum that 'personal is political' (Heywood, 2002, p. 62). In fact, women's movement for political rights started in the religious reforms in 1917 by the name of Women's Indian Association. Women's struggle for reforms in political rights and improving their property status is the off shoot of personal reforms. This struggle on the part of women implies that they needed those social and political reforms that affected them personally, covering the issues of rape, dowry and reforms in *sati*. This struggle has been in the backdrop of gender politics, a broader name of religious and regional politics that has been involved in marginalizing Indian women. The struggle by feminists implies that social pressures on women's bodies or putting in another way their individuality must be shifted to the more equal reforms for women. The issues have been mentioned earlier as the issues of dowry, social stigmatization of divorce, remarriages of widows or divorcee, etc, for, earlier, Ammu knew that her parents could not afford a large dowry and secondly after being divorced, she has lost her chance of remarriage. It is Ammu's stigmatized status that she is easily vulnerable to social pressure at home as well as from the ever present public opinion in the form of Keralite society, 'the constant, high, whining mewl of local disapproval' (p. 43). In the same line of thought, Ammu's assertion of her body is to be read in the personal and the political struggle of women; 'Ammu grew tired of their [the children's] proprietary handling of her. She wanted her body back. It was hers' (p. 222) and her rage at the public opinion at her divorce implies the struggle of political and social movements of Indian women as observed Tickell (2007).

The hints at Ammu's receiving wedding ring from her husband which she brings back with her after the devolution of her marriage is another perspective of legal, social and economic practices in the Indian society. This gift implies that a woman is only entitled to movable gifts at the time of her marriage from her husband. The hint at the transfer of this gift to Rahel also implies that a woman can transfer her wedding gift only to the female heiress, like her daughter. as 'she went to the village goldsmith and had her heavy wedding ring melted down and made in to bangle with snakeheads that she put away for Rahel' (p. 44). Through this message, Roy intends to cover the inheritance problem of an Indian woman. This chain or cycle goes unchallenged as after Ammu, Rahel replaces her mother and too gets deprived of her due status. Her problem is more serious as she lives at her grandmother's house and her property status remains unacknowledged as she belongs to a divorcee mother who had been struggling to find the surname for her children. The children legally belong to their father and Rahel's lack of legal standing implies that she has not inherited anything worthy from her father as again daughters remain deprived of property. It is the unrecognized status as a daughter again that she remains deprived from her right, even after her mother's death. 'Rahel grew up without...anybody to arrange a marriage for her. Without anybody who would pay her a dowry and therefore without an obligatory husband looming on her horizon' (p. 17). She remains destitute even doing a job in the States and the only possession Rahel possesses at her return from States is few hundred dollars and the same bangle which she had inherited from her mother. 'She [Rahel] had no plans. No Locust Stand I' (p. 188). This recurring phrase of Locust Stand I relating Ammu with Rahel, in fact, makes not only a literal connection between the novel but also connects the history of cultural and historical oppression of Indian women.

This context, i.e. the legal standing of women is to be studied in the light of pre-colonial customs and the postcolonial laws. According to Agarwal (1996), almost a half of the century has passed since Hindu Succession Act of 1956 has entitled Indian women the rights to property. Another point which is important to understand is that Hindu personal law, governing the inheritance rights through Hindu Succession Act 1956, as mentioned above is applicable to the Sikh communities, Jain and Buddhist communities in India. This Act exempts the Nambudri Brahims who can still rely on their customs to entitle women to property rights Agarwal (1996). What still is not clear in the context of *The God of Small Things* is whether the Syrian Christians, living within the customs of Nambudri Brahmins have completely been assimilated under the dominant Hindu order or have been selective in the cultural adaptation. The proposed suggestion on the part of the researcher is that cultural assimilation has might be selective in adapting to the profitable dominant customs suppressing the women in the access to the powerful resources and giving access to men to have control on the resources.

The features of Pakistani society with its multi-lingual and multi-cultural dimensions become problematic as far the women of Pakistan is concerned; problematic in the sense that Pakistan is a country where Islam is the religion of majority. Yet the various cultural forces exert their strong influence even on the religion. The extent or the limit of marginality from the center is even wider in case of Pakistan where sometimes regional and tribal code of conduct is dominant in the discourse of power than the prescriptions prescribed by the Quran, the all encompassing book of legal, economic and social conduct for Muslims. The social issues, raised in the context of *The Bride* above, are complex in the Pakistani context where regional forces as opposed to religious forces sometimes become dominant to marginalize the status of women. The fictional characters of Afshan, Zaitoon, Miriam, Carol and the women of Hira Mandi present the real problems of Pakistani women where they are doubly marginalized, at local and at cosmopolitan level. In fact the very complexity of the characters is the representation of the complexity of Pakistani social milieu. While reading *The God of Small Things* one notices that the cultural assimilation of the less dominant into the more dominant is pronounced wherever there is the dominant factor, such as cultural assimilation of the minority of Syrian Christians into the then, dominant Karalite value system and again the assimilation of Karalites and the Syrian

Christians into the dominant Hindu order. In the context of *The Bride* it becomes difficult to exactly pin point the position of the center as it really slips away from the grip; to determine which center is stronger; the religion or the culture. It is in this context of marginalization, in the ambiguity of the position of center and margin and even the number of centers and margins in the postcoloniality that Ashcroft (2001) referred to. According to him marginality implies multiple discourses of power working at the same time. And these centers of power work in a complex and confusing way. To infer from this definition by Ashcroft one perceives the complexity and confusion working in the Pakistani context of religion and culture; to specify whether religion is dominant or the culture. In this complex context of Pakistan, Ahmad (2010) opined that Pakistani women are the part of dominant patriarchal culture but this patriarchal oppression is difficult to determine as there exist a complex relationship between the forces of religion and culture, gender and class, and the forces of liberalism and conservatism etc. The divergent forces affect the lives of Pakistani women. Similarly the suppression of women in *The God of Small Things* has various shades but Roy centralizes Ammu as the object of suppression from different angles and all the female character follow the same strain of oppression such as socio and economic. But in case of Pakistani women, though Sidwa centralizes the character of Zaitoon, still the women in *The Bride* belong to different cultural milieu and hence the object of different cultural oppression. While Roy places the women of the same family and magnifies them to the cosmopolitan level showing the problems of Indian women at large, Sidwa takes different women from different cultures and presents their multi-pronged problems in the country where the dominant religion is Islam but age long traditions of different cultures pop their heads for influence. Shamsie (2011) testifies to this fact by comparing the Pakistani literature and its common themes with some of the features of South Asian literature, as it has common geographical implications for the area as well as the common colonial history. Along with this commonality Pakistani writers are also common in their themes of writings as it emerge from the Muslim identity as well. So while answering the question raised at the start of the discussion one cannot ignore the religious injunctions for the equality between men and women. Patel (2010) argued that Pakistani society is patriarchal with diverse socio-cultural background. Its social structure has been divided into three distinct hierarchical structures like urban, rural and tribal; the tribal localities governing their people through their own laws. In this environment women comprise the suppressed segment of society.

An overview of the Pakistani law encompassing the legal and economic issues is important to discuss here. Tracing the legal history of Pakistan it is essential to go through the colonial history before the independence on Pakistan. The English colonizers remained non interfering in the local laws which have been governing their people before the British arrival. Religious laws along with the customary laws were applied for the people living in their different localities conforming to their customs and traditions. This implies that the personal law encompassing the issues of marriages, divorce, inheritance practices, dowry, maintenance etc, governing the people was not changed by the colonizers and the indigenous people were left free to follow their own laws and statutes and there were the Hindu, the Muslim and the Christian laws depending on the faith respectively. The Muslims of the pre-Independence were governed by the same laws enacted by the English colonizers. This law was called the Anglo-Muhammadan Law, which according to A. K. Brohi (as cited in Patel, 2010) was a compromise between the liberal and the orthodox forces. Later these laws were reformed after independence which were named as Muslim Personal Law (Shariat) which was applicable to all Muslims according the sects, except the tribal areas and from then onwards this law is known as Muslim Personal Law. According to this law women are entitled to maintenance, as a daughter from her father and as a wife from her husband, observed Patel (2010). In the same context, i.e. legal and economic standing, a Muslim woman is entitled to the share in the property according to her status, being a daughter and being a wife. The son inherits a larger portion of property from his father, and the daughter inherits the half of the brother's. It means that Islam ensures a woman's right to property. Another thing which is important to understand in Pakistani context is the presence of tribal law which governs its people in its own right. Generally, according to all schools of Islamic law women are entitled to share in immovable property Agarwal (1996). What is important to understand in Pakistani context is that customary laws have also been operating along with the Muslim Personal Law. The purpose of describing such legal details is to inquire as to why women are deprived of their legal and economic rights as the context of *The Bride* provides. Pakistani government, according to Agarwal (1996) has entitled Pakistani women the right to property through West Pakistan Shariat Act of 1962 which makes religious injunctions to supersede the customs governing the legal rights and women's access to the landed property. One reason for such deprivation according to Agarwal (1996) is the gap between the prescriptions of Islam and the real situation or the practice among the Muslims belonging to diverse culture. The reason for such a deviation from the prescription of Shariat is the proximity of Muslims with their Hindu neighbours. The exclusion of Hindu women from the inheritance of the property naturally affected the Muslims living close to each other and hence the practice became the custom. Another reason is that the British colonizers gave principal importance to the customs governing their concerned localities or regions to ensure the colonizer's stronghold on the tribal belt; for tribal security depended on the landed property hence ultimately excluding women from the inheritance. Punjabi tribal code also depended on such customs of inheritance. However various changes were brought in the laws enacted by the British in favour of women but the loopholes remained. The West Pakistan Muslim Personal Law Application Act of 1962 extended the Shariat as the basis of personal law to the whole of West Pakistan except the tribal areas of the then NWFP, now KPK as the tribal areas have their own legal system the *jarga* system, a tribal judicial system comprising the elders of the community where individual as well collective issues are settled through *Pukhtoonwali,* the tribal code, observed Jafri (2008).

Viewing the things in the context of *The Bride* all female characters are marginalized legally, economically and socially. Interestingly the strains of marginalization are hard with the start of marriages in Pakistan as Sidwa comments that marriages are the high point for Pakistani women and Patel (2010) opined that marriages have the ultimate and lasting effects on women. Afshan, Zaitoon and Hamida have no legal standing as being tribal women Afshan and Zaitoon are contracted into marriage without their consent (Zaitoon is fancied into the tribal life by her father). Their bartering as commodity itself implies that they have no economic rights if any under the tribal laws.

Same economic deprivation and social stigmatization is present in the women belonging to singing and dancing class of society. While analyzing the things from legal, economic and social issues it becomes clear that Pakistani women in *The Bride* are marginalized in every respect. The cultural and religious assimilation in the context of Pakistan is mixed as somewhere the customs and tradition preceded where they have been in the dominant order while in some places the religion of Islam with its stronghold dominated.

This discussion and analysis of the Pakistani as well as Indian society carried out in the context of *The God of Small Things* and *The Bride*, leads to the issue of marginalization from local to the global perspective; firstly, taking the issue from the subcontinent to South Asia; and secondly from South Asia to the world at large. Studying the novels in the light of Eastern feminist critics such as Spivak and situating this analysis parallel to the Western feminist criticism such as Showalter and Simone de Beauvoir, it becomes clear that gender discrimination is beyond space and time; Western women as well as Eastern women both have faced such a discrimination. But by analyzing the edge from various centers, the centers of imperialism, patriarchy, neocolonialism etc., South Asian women are particularly important as they share the heritage of colonialism as well. It is in this context, the difference between the Western feminism and the Eastern feminism, as proposed by Spivak is relevant here. She argues that Third World women as against their counterpart First World women are marginalized from various centers which she referred to as double marginalization, not only from the patriarchal structures, or the inherent pre-colonial legal system but also from the centers formed after colonialism. Therefore, the difference that Spivak talked about, between the Western and the Eastern women is important here. It is in this context that Spivak takes the stance for Indian women in particular; and South Asian women in general and says that 'our identity is without a fixed center and inherently unstable' (Bertens, 2008, p. 171). In other words South Asian women are encountering multiple forces that are marginalizing them. In the same strain, while discussing the marginalization of women, Mohanty (1988) rejected the Western idea of homogenous group of women belonging to the Third World women and depicted social and economic system as the causes of marginality in Third World developing countries. According to Ahmad (2010) the heterogeneity in Pakistani women's context is important as they are carrying Muslim identity with them as well. So South Asian women are facing social, economic and political problems because they are the in the constraints of both pre and postcolonial legal and social order. This heterogeneity on the part of South Asian women is also clearly evident from the textual analysis of the novels under study. Carol, the American Pakistani bride in *The Bride* is critical as well as unaware of most of culture and the value system of Pakistani society. Similarly, Larry McCaslin, Rahel's American husband is unable to understand the way Rahel behaves, 'He didn't know that in some places, like the country that Rahel came from, various kinds of despair competed for primacy' (p. 19). This difference of the social values between the Eastern and Western societies makes the researcher to infer that South Asian value system has affected the lives of women from various angles and this comparison of East with West according to the researcher might be intentional on the part of Roy and Sidwa. This analysis further testifies to the far reaching effects as discussed in the context of marginalization of female characters in the novels under study, particularly, and of the South Asian women generally.

# Chapter V

## Conclusions

Is it history, culture or religion that pushes women to the margin? Is it the game of isms, the capitalism, in the form of market economy or globalization; Marxism, the German, the Russian or the Indian version; Fascism; or the liberalism, that make women suppressed? Is it the pre-colonial customs or the postcolonial laws that make the women get to the margins? Or, what is it that makes all the women characters oppressed in the context of *The God of Small Things* and *The Bride?* The research findings of the data gathered from primary and secondary sources are presented with reference to each of the research questions. Feminist criticism, both Eastern and Western, such as proposed by Showalter and Spivak has been taken into consideration; postcolonial theory and Marxist theoretical perspective have been employed to solve the research questions. Bringing the issues into the spotlight of the said methodology, the research questions which have been raised in the Introduction will be answered and explained.

Through discussion and analysis of the marginalized position of female characters in the novels under study, *The God of Small Things* and *The Bride*, the first question as to why South Asian societies are particularly exposed to marginalization is finally reached. South Asia is a region where various forces of patriarchy, imperialism, neo-imperialism and globalization converge. Its history is also marred by the colonizing agenda of the First World countries to civilize the otherwise uncivilized people. In such a scenario women are marginalized. In fact, they are doubly marginalized, as the patriarchy in the form of institutions such as family, society and state and religion, culture and customs has been dominating them for ages; and colonization; imperial and neo-imperial forces in the form of laws marginalize their already constrained positions. Therefore, unlike the social structure of European societies South Asia is particularly exposed to the marginalizing forces.

It is in this context that the present project has carried out the research on the female characters of *The God of Small Things* and *The Bride*. All female characters are marginalized, no matter to which class they belong. From Mammachi, to the female factory workers and the prostitutes in *The God of Small Things* and from Carol, American bride to Zaitoon and the dancing women in *The Bride* all are marginalized; and they are marginalized not from a single center, whether it is the patriarchy or the colonizers, but marginalized from the multiple centers of power. Through the discussion and analysis it is concluded that female characters, in the context the novels, being the part of South Asian society have been under the influence of double marginalization.

As to the question that how far economic rights in particular and social, political, legal and religious rights in general could have determined the rightful status of female characters, I have concluded that had female characters had the economic rights, they could have been at the bargaining and contesting position. Ammu could have been able to fight back the marginalizing forces of Chacko at home and later on, the employer's at the societal level. Sharing the ancestral property with her brother she could have been able to avoid the destitute which is forced upon her and her children. Mammachi, in spite of the owner of the property could have enjoyed the control of it. The *locus standi*, the dominant theme of *The God of Small Things*, which all female characters lacked, could have been the powerful force in determining their sound position, both at the family and at the societal level.

As to the social, political, and religious rights, through discussion and analysis, I have reached to the conclusion that entitlement to personal rights leads to the entitlement of political right; access to personal rights leads to public resources.

As to the third question, the role of cultural assimilation in marginalizing female characters, I conclude that cultural assimilation in the context of *The God of Small Things* and *The Bride*, is equally responsible. As South Asia is a culturally diverse region, it absorbed the customs, traditions and the value system of various communities; Syrian Christians, Roman Catholics, Hindus, Muslims, tribal communities merging into the dominant religions, etc.; all these cultural changes affected the position of women in one way or the other. The liberty which the women enjoyed under the pre-colonial customs was curtailed under the postcolonial laws; or the amendments in the postcolonial legal systems went unrecognized under the pre-colonial customs. Similarly, the assimilation of culture and religion is also responsible for female marginalization; the assimilation of the cultural values of Nayar and Namboodri tribes in to Syrian Christians' value system and the assimilation of Syrian Christians in to Hinduism, in the context of *The God of Small Things* and the assimilation of tribal values into Islam and vice versa, in the context of *The Bride*. In other words, women in South Asian society have been affected by cultural absorption. The Hindu Marriage Act, 1955, the Hindu Succession Act, 1956, the Dowry Prohibition Act, 1961,

Sati Act, etc, in India and Muslim Family Laws Ordinances 1961 in Pakistan are the steps to reform the pre-colonial customs.

Lastly, the question whether ideology of the ruling class in the form of religion, laws, politics etc. can be manipulated in favour of women; whether the institutions of church, the government, the police in *The God of Small Things* could have been changed or reformed in favour of women characters in the novels. The answer is that improving the class of women in a society, recognizing equal position of women, the hegemony of the ruling ideas can be challenged; or if the women do not reconcile to the dominant ideology. Had female characters been granted economic rights they would have been in a position of bargaining and contesting for their rights. If they had the 'safe edge' as Roy reminds the readers again and again or Sidwa implies in the depiction of her characters, they could have been at a socially acceptable positions.

# Bibliography

Abbas, T. & Idris, M. M. (2011). *Honour, violence, women and Islam*. New York: Routledge.

Agarwal, B. (1996). *A field of one's own: Gender and land rights in South Asia*. New Delhi: Cambridge University Press.

Ahmad, I. (2013). The conquered land: A feminist reading of Bapsi Sidwa's *The Pakistani Bride*. *The Criterion: An International Journal in English*, *4*, 1-3.

Ahmad, S. (Ed). (2010). *Pakistani women: Multiple locations and competing narratives*. Karachi: Oxford University Press.

Ahsan, A. (2008). *The Indus saga and the making of Pakistan*. Islamabad: The Army Press.

Al Quaderi, G. G. & Islam, S. M. (2011). Complicity and resistance: Women in Arundhati Roy's The God of Small Things. *Journal of Postcolonial Culture and Societies, 2*(4), 62-78.

Alvi, D. S., Baseer, A. & Zahoor, S. (2012). Bapsi Sidwa's The Bride: An alternative view point in Pakistani literature. *Interdisciplinary Journal of Contemporary Research in Business, 3*(10), 87-92.

Ashcroft, B., Griffiths, G. & Tiffin, H. (2001). *Key concepts in postcolonial studies*. London: Routledge.

Ashcroft, B., Griffiths, G. & Tiffin, H. (2002). *The empire writes back*. New York: Routledge.

Axford, B., Huggins, R. & Turner. (1997). *Politics: An introduction*. New York: Routledge.

Barkty, S. (1979). On psychological oppression. *Southwestern Journal of Philosophy, 10*(1), 190.

Bertens, H. (2008). *Literary theory: The basics*. Routledge: New York.

Bose, S. & Jalal, A. (1998). *Modern South Asia: History, culture, political economy*. New York: Routledge.

Brian, P. (2003). *Modern South Asian literature in English*. Greenwood Press: USA.

Butler, J. (1986). Sex and gender in Simone de Beauvoir's The Second Sex. *Yale French Studies, 72*, 35-49.

Chambers, C. (2011). A comparative approach to Pakistani fiction in English. *Journal of Postcolonial Writing, 47*(2), 122-134.

Chattopadhya, B. (2009). (Ed). *A social history of early India*. New Delhi: Dorling Kindersley Pvt. Ltd.

Dodiya, J. (2006). *Parsi English novel*. New Delhi: Sarup & sons.

Dodiya, J. (2006).*Critical essay on Indian writing in English*. New Delhi: Sarup & sons.

Forbes, G. (1998). *Women in modern India*. Cambridge: Cambridge University Press.

Freud, S. (1920). *A general introduction to psychoanalysis*. New York: Horace Liveright.

Furguson, R. (1990). *Out there: Marginalization and contemporary culture*. USA: MIT Press.

Giles, M. (2011). Postcolonial Gothic and *The God of Small Things*: The haunting of India's past. *Postcolonial Text, 6,* 1-15.

Gonsalves, L. (2011). *Women and human rights*. New Delhi: APH Publishing Corporation.

Heywood, A. (2002). *Politics*. New York: Palgrave.

Hussain, Y. (2005). *Writing diaspora: South Asian women, culture and ethnicity*. Hampshire: Ashgate Publishing Ltd.

Jafri, H. A. (2008). *Honour killing: Dilemma, ritual, understanding*. Oxford: Oxford University Press.

Jalal, A. (1995). *Democracy and authoritarianism in South Asia: A comparative and historical perspective*. Lahore: Sang-e-Meel Publication.

Khan, F. A. (2013). Man woman relationship: Crisis of moral values a study of Bapsi Sidwa's *The Pakistani Bride*. *International*

*Journal of English and Literature, 3,* 156-164.

Khan, F. (1995). Indian Subcontinent: Pakistani writing in English: 1947- to the present: A survey. *Wasafiri, 10*(21), 58-61.

Lane, J. R. (2006). *Fifty key literary theorist.* New York: Routledge.

Lener, G. (1975). Placing women in history: Definitions and challenges. *Feminist Studies Inc, 3*, 5-14.

Lener, G. (1986). *The creation of patriarchy.* New York: Oxford University Press.

Marwah, S. F. A. (2008). When I raised my head again. Feminism and the female body in Bapsi Sidwa's novels *The Pakistani Bride* and *The Cracking India* (Master thesis, University of Oslo).

<http://www.duo.no/bitstream/handle/10850/25551/MasterxAnexMarwah.pdf?sequence=2>

Mishra, B. (2006). (Ed). *Critical responses to feminism*. New Delhi: Sarup & sons.

Moghadam, M. V. (2007). (Ed). *From patriarchy to empowerment: Women's participation, movements and rights in the Middle East, North Africa and South Asia*. New York: Syracuse University Press.

Mohanty, C. (1988). Under Western eyes: Feminist scholarship and colonial discourse. *Palgrave macmillan, 30*(1), 61-88.

Mullaney, J. (2002). *Arundhati Roy's The God of Small Things: A reader's guide (continuum contemporaries)*.

New York: The Continuum International Publishing Group.

Nanda, S. (2012). Women as the Oppressed in *The God of Small Things*. *The Criterion: An International Journal in English, 3*(3), 1-7.

Nazari, F. (2013). Revisiting colonial legacy in Arundhati Roy's *The God of Small Things*. *Journal of Educational and Social Research, 3,* 199-210.

Nelson, S. E. (2000). *Asian American novelist: A biographical critical sourcebook*. USA: Greenwood Press.

Olsson, A. (2011). Arundhati Roy: Reclaiming voices on the margins in *The God of Small Things*. Bachelor thesis. <www.diva-portal.org/smash/get/diva2:394114/FULLTEXT01.pdf>

Pandey, B. (2001). *Indian women novelist in English*. New Delhi: Sarup & sons.

Patchay, S. (2007). Pickled histories, bottled stories: Recuperative narratives in *The God of Small Things. Journal of Literary Studies*, *17*(3-4), 145-160.

Pateman, C. (1990). *The order of women: Democracy, feminism and political theory.* California: Stanford University Press.

Pateman, C. (1988). *The social contract.* California: Stanford University Press.

Patel, R. (2010). *Gender equality and women's empowerment in Pakistan.* Karachi: Oxford University Press.

Prasad, N. A. (2004). (Ed). *Arundhati Roy's The God of Small Things*: *A critical appraisal.* New Delhi: Sarup & sons:

Rosaldo, Z. M. & Lamphere L. (1974). (Ed). *Women, culture and society.* California: Stanford University Press.

Roy, A. (2005). *The God of Small Things: A novel of social commitment.* New Delhi: Atlantic Publishers.

Roy, A. (1997). *The God of Small Things.* London: Flamingo.

Saeed, F. (2011). *Taboo!: The hidden culture of a red light area.* Karachi: Oxford University Press.

Sanga, C. J. (2003). *South Asian novelists in English: An A-Z guide.* USA: Greenwood Press.

Shamsie, M. (2011). Duality and diversity in Pakistani English literature. *Journal of postcolonial writing, 47* (2), 119-121.

Shamsie, M.. (2007). Complexities of home and homeland in Pakistani English poetry and fiction. In Lal Malashri & Kumar, Paul Sukrita (Eds.), *Interpreting homes in South Asian literature*. Delhi: Dorling Kindersley Pvt. Ltd.

Showalter, Elaine. (1981). Feminist criticism in the wilderness. *Chicago Journal, 8* (2), 179-205.

Sidwa, B. (2012). *The Bride.* Lahore: ILQA Publications. (Original work published in 1983)

Singh, P. R. (2005). *Bapsi Sidwa*. New Delhi: IVI Publishing House.

Sinha, S. (2008). *Postcolonial women writers: New perspectives*. New Delhi: Atlantic Publishers.

Thormann, J. (2003). The Ethical Subject in *The God of Small Things*. *Journal for the Psychoanalysis of Culture and Society*, *8*(2), 299-307.

Tickell, A. (2007). *Arundhati Roy's The God of Small Things*.USA: Routledge.

Tiwary, N. & Chandra, R.D.N. (2009). New historicism and Arundhati Roy's work. *Journal of Literature, Culture and Media Studies*, *6*, 79-96.

Wong, P. M. & Hassan, Z. (2004). *The Fiction of South Asian in North America and the Caribbean*. North Carolina: McFarland & Company, Inc.

Printed in Great Britain
by Amazon